SIMPLY
# SUSTAINABLE

# SIMPLY SUSTAINABLE

Moving Toward Plastic-Free,
Low-Waste Living

LILY CAMERON

Photographs by Aubrie Pick

10
TEN SPEED PRESS
California | New York

For Gigi

# Contents

# GOING PLASTIC-FREE(ISH)

I never considered myself part of the plastic problem. I grew up in California, the land of hippies and tree huggers, and my parents bought groceries in reusable totes long before plastic bag bans. I knew littering was wrong and recycling was good, and we even had an outdoor compost pile for kitchen scraps.

As an adult, I felt good about my environmental efforts. After graduating from the University of California, Berkeley, I landed a job managing public relations for clean technology startups in the solar, energy storage, and water purification industries. I also rode public transportation to work or walked, ate a vegetarian diet, and lobbied my landlord to add a compost bin to our building. I knew climate change was a serious issue and scoffed at the drivers of gas-guzzling SUVs.

It wasn't until I read about the zero-waste movement that I realized I could be doing better (like, *a lot*). I learned about a no-nonsense French woman, Bea Johnson, who fit an entire year's worth of her family's trash into a single 8-ounce Le Parfait jar. Seeing how little waste she produced made me reflect on my lifestyle, and when I looked closer, I didn't like what I saw.

My fridge was filled with premade salads in plastic clamshells, foam take-out containers, and leftover bits of produce and cheese bundled in plastic wrap. I loved shopping and my closet was overflowing with fast fashion that I replaced often. My bathroom drawers and shower were littered with expensive shampoos, serums, and other fancy products that promised flawless skin and long shiny hair. I guzzled lattes from a disposable to-go cup the size of my head each morning on my way to work.

Could I really call myself an environmentalist while stuffing massive garbage bags in the bin each week? Learning about the zero-waste movement was my wake-up call, and I was determined to make the switch to a plastic-free lifestyle. My fiancé and I had just returned from a three-month road trip where we backpacked through the Pacific Northwest and decided it was the perfect time to quit plastic cold turkey. I couldn't wait to fit an entire year's worth of trash into a Mason jar.

I used up the last roll of paper towels and replaced it with reusable cloth rags. I switched from enormous to-go cups of coffee to loose-leaf tea bought in bulk and brewed at home (after discovering coffee made my skin break out). I found a body wash that could double as a shampoo and bought refills at a natural foods co-op with my own glass jar. I scoured the San Francisco Bay Area for ingredients to make toothpaste, lotion, and sunscreen from scratch.

Minimalism, a skill I developed while backpacking, became an incredibly helpful method for reducing waste. My home had become cluttered and disorganized after years of moving around the Bay Area. I was a sucker for kitschy decor and vintage clothing from flea markets and thrift stores (which I thought were a bargain), but in reality, they took up valuable space, money, and the time required to care for these items. Purging unused belongings helped reset my consumption patterns and made me realize I often bought things out of boredom—not necessity. I became more cautious when making new purchases, investigating what materials each product was made from and how it would be disposed of at the end of its useful life.

With my newly minimal home and dedication to plastic-free living, my household garbage was shrinking, but I was also encountering some setbacks. For one, I couldn't find many of the reusable products I was looking for to replace disposables, such as a wood dish brush and cloth produce bags, and when I bought them online, they were shipped with wasteful plastic packaging. And, although my garbage was decreasing, it was nowhere near being able to fit into a Mason jar. I was wracked with eco-guilt every time I made a misstep and starting to lose steam. Zero waste didn't feel like fun; it felt like sacrifice and extra work.

My approach shifted after a yoga class (*I know*, cliché), during which the instructor urged us not to compare our practice to other yogis around us. I realized that to make plastic-free living sustainable, I needed to focus on *my* journey and stop measuring my progress against the seemingly perfect lifestyles shown on Instagram. To make it work for the long haul, zero waste needed to be adaptable and forgiving, especially when life threw me a curveball (looking at you, COVID-19). I let go of the idea of squeezing my trash into a jar and started to focus on the wins—remembering to bring a reusable cup to my local cafe; successfully making All-Purpose Cleaner (page 97) from natural ingredients; and finding a plastic-free deodorant that actually worked.

This journey eventually led my husband and me to leave our corporate jobs to launch Wild Minimalist, a curated shop for zero-waste essentials with plastic-free shipping. Our family store has grown alongside the zero-waste movement and motivated me to share our journey on our blog, including tips, recipes, and the inevitable daily struggles.

While I am proud to participate in the zero-waste movement, I've also become more aware of its limitations and flaws. The trash jar has been an incredibly motivating symbol for many to reduce waste. For others, it's intimidating, unrealistic, and at its worst, exclusionary. Having access to bulk groceries, cleaning, and beauty supplies, and being able to afford reusable replacements for disposable products is a privilege that not everyone shares. Many communities, especially communities of color (who bear the highest impacts of climate change), have been practicing resourcefulness and conservation for centuries, yet these same communities have been largely excluded from the environmental movement and zero-waste conversation. I believe it's important to expand the definition and depictions of a zero-waste lifestyle in order to mobilize diverse participants, while also taking a critical look at the intersection of race and environmental issues (check out some recommended reading on page 201).

My goal with this book is to share the joy and beauty of living a *mostly* plastic-free lifestyle, and to show there is no perfect one-size-fits-all approach. It's virtually impossible to eliminate 100 percent of plastic from our lives, and there still may be some products or practices you're not ready to part with, but with some preparation and a little mindfulness, you can drastically reduce waste and make your home more minimalist, inviting, and beautiful.

For the plastic-free movement to make a truly positive impact, we need a lot of people reducing waste imperfectly, not a handful of people fitting trash into a jar. So, if you're like me—you care about the environment and want to curb plastic in a manageable (and fun) way—you've come to the right place.

# What Is *Zero* Waste?

I'm going to venture to say *most* people don't want to harm the environment. We try to do our part by dutifully recycling or buying "eco-friendly" cleaning products, but we're also busy, overcommitted, and just want to live our lives without feeling as though we're depriving ourselves for the sake of environmentalism. Balancing careers, chores, friends, and family, and still carving out time for self-care can be tough. When people hear *zero* waste it can sound intimidating and prescriptive, like adding extra work onto an already crowded plate.

But, what if I told you going zero-waste will simplify life, save time and money, and even add beauty? (And yes, help save the environment.) Try not to get too caught up in the terminology *zero* waste or plastic *free*—producing absolutely zero plastic waste isn't possible unless you grow all your own food and pretty much remove yourself from society. For some people, it's about fitting their trash into a Mason jar, and for many others (including yours truly) it's about taking gradual, intentional steps to reduce the waste sent to landfill. You do this by adopting a set of practices and principles that make waste reduction simple, time-saving, affordable, and fun. But, before we dive in, let's pause to review the advantages of ditching plastic waste.

# Reasons to Ditch Plastic

**Preserve the environment.** The very advantages of plastic that make it so ubiquitous—it's lightweight, durable, disposable—come at the disadvantage of the environment and wildlife. Plastic is showing up everywhere—from the deepest trenches of the ocean to the highest mountain peaks—and it *never* biodegrades. Rather, it breaks down into tiny pieces called microplastics that get mixed into the soil and ocean. This is particularly harmful to marine animals that mistake plastic for food, which then eventually makes its way back into our food chain.

**Add beauty.** Minimalists love to quote British textile designer William Morris, "Have nothing in your houses that you do not know to be useful, or believe to be beautiful." The fact is, plastic isn't pretty—it's cheap and flimsy and designed to be thrown away. When our homes are filled with single-use products, we start treating all our belongings as if they're disposable. By comparison, reusable items made from wood, glass, metal, and natural fabrics are a pleasure to use and look at, and can even make mundane chores a little more joyful. One of my favorite discoveries was swapping a plastic sponge for a wood dish brush—I love the way the brush looks beside my sink, and that I no longer have smelly sponge hands after doing dishes (gross).

**Protect your health and communities.** Plastic is contaminating the water we drink, the food we consume, and the air we breathe. It presents distinct risks to our health at every stage of its lifecycle, from the pollution emitted during manufacturing to the toxins leached into our food while cooking. There is growing evidence that all this plastic exposure has an adverse effect on our health—mimicking hormones, disrupting the reproductive system, and potentially causing cancer. Communities of color are disproportionately located near plastic refineries and landfills, meaning they are most impacted by the resulting pollution—an example of environmental racism.

**Save money.** Many people worry that switching to a zero-waste lifestyle will be expensive. It's true that reusable products aren't cheap compared to disposables—they're made from higher quality materials and are designed to last. At its core, zero waste is about being mindful, resourceful, and using what you already have. You will save money by buying less, buying secondhand, and selling belongings that no longer serve you. Also, consider how much money you could save if you never bought a disposable product again—no more plastic sandwich bags, cutlery, plastic cling wrap, paper towels, etc. It adds up.

## THE BAD NEWS

### 91%

Of all plastic waste ever produced, only 9 percent has been recycled–91 percent has gone to landfill.

### 46,000

Plastic comprises 90 percent of ocean trash–with 46,000 pieces of plastic per square mile.

### 70,000

The average person eats more than 70,000 particles of microplastics each year.

### 500–1,000

It takes between 500 and 1,000 years for plastic to break down.

### 6:1

The Great Pacific Garbage Patch is twice the size of Texas, with pieces of plastic outnumbering marine life 6:1.

### 2050

If we don't curb plastic waste, there will be more plastic than fish by weight in the ocean by 2050.

## THE GOOD NEWS

Although the statistics above are alarming, I believe it's important to stay optimistic and focus on how we can make impactful change. The zero-waste movement is growing and sending a message to corporations, politicians, and peers that our environment is precious and there is a strong market for plastic-free alternatives. Here are a few more reasons to stay hopeful.

### 2021

The European Union plans to ban single-use plastic items, such as straws, food containers, and cotton buds, by 2021.

### 400

In the United States, more than 400 cities and states have banned or taxed plastic bags to reduce waste.

### 34

The African continent leads the world in plastic bag regulations, with 34 countries adopting taxes or bans.

### 2020

IKEA has pledged to phase out all single-use plastic products by 2020, including plates, cups, and straws.

### 4 million

Trader Joe's is implementing packaging changes to remove four million pounds of plastic from stores annually.

### 2018

In 2018, Seattle became the first major city to ban plastic straws. Many cities have followed suit.

# 5 Rs of Zero Waste

We've covered the advantages of reducing our plastic dependence and going zero waste, but how does it actually work in real life? A zero-waste lifestyle is influenced by the 5 Rs of waste reduction—*refuse, reduce, reuse, recycle,* and *rot*. The order of the waste hierarchy is intentional and is meant to prioritize how we eliminate waste. It may surprise you that recycling, while important, is one of the *least* effective ways to ditch plastic . . . but I'm getting ahead of myself.

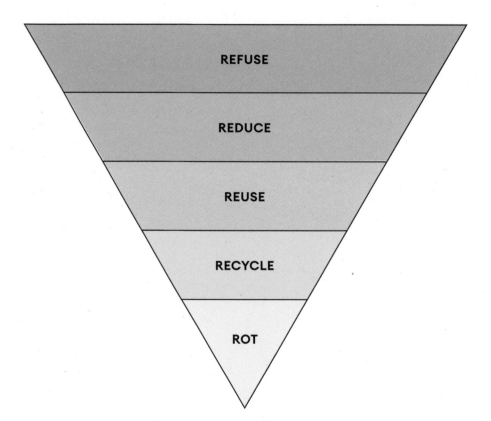

**Refuse.** The first R not only has the biggest impact on waste reduction, it's one of the easiest to implement. Start your journey to zero waste simply by refusing single-use products, like plastic bags, straws, cutlery, take-out boxes, and to-go cups. When you dine out, request no plastic straw. When you buy groceries or home supplies, skip the bag (plastic or otherwise) and carry it out by hand or in a reusable tote. When grabbing a cup of coffee, request a real cup versus the to-go variety or bring a reusable mug from home.

Another way to refuse is to decline "freebies"—business cards, junk mail, flyers, samples, coupons, party favors, swag, and more. It may sound simple, but when someone offers you something free, you're allowed to say, "No, thanks." In a society where accepting free things has become the norm, saying *no* can feel impolite. We often say *yes* because we don't want to seem rude, but accepting freebies reinforces wasteful practices and creates a demand for more disposable items.

---

**Reduce.** When we consume fewer things, we reduce our impact on the environment. Of course, if we consumed nothing, there would be no trash. But being zero waste isn't about depriving yourself and never buying anything again, it's about being a more mindful consumer and resetting wasteful spending habits. Shopping can give us an endorphin rush similar to sex or working out, and we can become addicted to the pleasure of buying something new. A good way to reset is to pause before buying something—it can be as little as 24 hours or as challenging as a month-long spending freeze. After some time has passed, you'll often discover you no longer want the item or have found something else to repurpose in its place.

Pausing before buying something new also gives us the opportunity to *precycle*—to consider a product's lifecycle and its impact on the environment before it is purchased. Single-use products are cheaply made and designed to break so we keep buying new ones. We vote with our wallets when we shop, and when we favor reusable, recyclable, and compostable products over single-use, packaged products, we send a message—your business does not align with my values.

**Reuse.** It's time to rethink the disposable culture we live in. Many everyday items are designed to be used once or twice before they're tossed, and we're quick to replace broken or damaged products. Reuse is extending a product's usefulness before it's recycled or sent to landfill. By reusing a product, even once, you reduce the waste that would come from manufacturing, transporting, and eventually disposing of an additional item. Finding a way to reuse objects helps foster creativity—it can be as simple as converting an emptied pasta sauce jar into a vase or storage container for bulk food. We can also extend a product's useful life by repairing clothing, shoes, electronics, and furniture when they become damaged.

Some other ways to reuse and support our local community include purchasing secondhand, borrowing, and renting. Buy apparel and housewares from the local thrift store, check out books from the library, borrow tools from a neighbor, or rent a dress for a special occasion.

---

**Recycle.** Here's the thing about recycling: it's a good place to start, and a bad place to stop. I used to think I was doing my part to save the environment by recycling alone. What I didn't consider is that recycling just delays what is sent to landfill. Of course, recycling is more eco-friendly than tossing something straight into the trash, but it can also be a resource-intensive process that requires energy, labor, and fuel—a burden often outsourced to other countries.

On a positive note, glass and metal can be recycled indefinitely, without a loss of quality. By contrast, most plastic can be recycled only once before losing its integrity and being sent to landfill. Also, most plastic has to be downcycled—a plastic water bottle can be turned into a lower quality material like carpet fiber, but it cannot be turned into a new water bottle. Try to buy fewer products made from plastic and be diligent about recycling any plastic you do use. Look into local collection sites for hard-to-recycle items such as batteries and broken electronics (see my recycling guide on page 192).

NOTE ON RECYCLING SYMBOLS
The recycling symbol on packaging doesn't always mean it's recyclable. The symbol is often used to identify the type of plastic or may just mean the packaging contains recycled materials. Always check your local waste guidelines to see what they accept.

**Rot.** The US Environmental Protection Agency estimates that more than 28 percent of household waste can be composted. But food sent to landfill eventually breaks down, *right*? As it turns out, organic materials such as food, paper, and plants become trapped under layers of garbage and do not receive the required sunlight and oxygen to decompose. This creates methane—a destructive greenhouse gas that's 25 percent more potent than carbon monoxide.

Adding a compost bin to your home will help keep organic materials out of landfill and return nutrients to the soil—it will also drastically reduce your household waste. If you already compost food scraps, take it a step further and compost paper towels and napkins, cotton balls, dog fur, and more (each chapter offers suggestions for compostable household items). If your city doesn't offer a compost service, look into starting a home compost (for a guide to compost methods, see page 193).

---

**COMPOSTING TIPS**

**Choose wisely.** You'll need something big enough to hold scraps for a day or two (or more depending on how often you plan to add them to the compost). No need to buy a special container—try repurposing a chipped enamel pot, a plastic storage container, or an empty ice-cream tub.

**Determine location.** We keep our compost container on the counter, within easy reach while we're cooking. This also reminds us to empty it regularly, but many people prefer to store theirs out of sight under the sink. If you plan to empty it less frequently and are worried about smells, store scraps in the freezer.

**Skip the liner.** Many municipal waste facilities don't have the capability to process "biodegradable" plastic bags. Skip the liner and use a container that can be washed easily with soap or placed in the dishwasher. If you prefer to use a liner, reuse a paper bag, which will break down easily.

# ALSO, *PLEASE* STOP WISHCYCLING

Recycling can be tricky. We might be uncertain about what materials our packaging is made from, confused by ambiguous symbols, or simply *wish* that something could be recyclable. Brush up on your local waste guidelines to ensure you are recycling accepted items, and not *wishcycling* items you're unsure about, including:

**Broken crockery.** Broken plates, ceramics, porcelain, wineglasses, and Pyrex have a different chemical composition compared to recyclable glass products and belong in the trash.

**Compostable plastic.** Unfortunately, most compostable plastic must be sent to an offsite facility for processing. Check your local waste guidelines to see if they accept it.

**Diapers.** Hopefully, it's no surprise that dirty diapers don't belong in recycling. Some diapers are compostable, but they usually have to be picked up by a diaper service for processing.

**Dirty containers.** Dirty peanut butter jars and wine bottles can contaminate an entire truckload of recyclables. Containers don't have to be *perfectly* clean, but they should be rinsed and washed with soap if they're greasy.

**Freezer boxes.** Freezer food boxes and ice-cream cartons contain a plastic coating to prevent freezer burn. This also stops the box or carton from breaking down in the recycling process. They should be thrown away.

**Gift wrap.** Metallic wrapping paper, glittery cards, and decorative ribbons do not belong in recycling and can contaminate an entire load. Find a way to reuse them or throw them away.

**Milk cartons.** Gable-topped milk and juice cartons are made from a paper-plastic composite to prevent leaks. Although some municipalities accept cartons in curbside pick-up, many do not.

**Plastic bags.** Plastic bags can clog machines. Type your zip code into PlasticFilmRecycling.com to find a soft plastic recycling drop-off near you.

**Pizza boxes.** If it has grease stains, it doesn't belong in recycling. Lucky for pizza lovers, food-soiled cardboard and paper can be composted, including used paper towels and napkins.

**Receipts.** Although thermal receipts are made from paper, they are often coated with bisphenol A (BPA), a suspected carcinogen. When receipts are recycled, the BPA gets mixed into the paper pulp and contaminates products made from it.

**Shredded paper.** Shredded documents and small bits of paper can fall through the cracks and even clog equipment. Compost paper scraps instead.

**Small metal.** Although small pieces of metal are technically recyclable, they can be hard to detect by machinery. Keep soda tabs attached to the can or drop them inside. Save shreds of aluminum foil until they form a ball the size of your fist, then recycle.

**Take-out boxes.** Most paper take-out boxes are lined with a plastic film that makes them nonrecyclable. They can only be composted if they're 100 percent paper.

**To-go cups.** Most to-go cups are lined with leakproof plastic that makes them difficult to recycle. The cardboard heat sleeve and plastic lid may be recyclable (check local guidelines).

# How to Start Living Zero Waste

**Start with *why*.** There is no wrong reason to reduce plastic waste. Most people point to climate change, which is certainly a good motivation. But, to be honest, one of my biggest incentives for reducing waste was that I craved simplicity—having fewer things (including waste) helps me feel more organized and less anxious. I also just like the way it looks. I enjoy cooking from my (mostly) plastic-free pantry, washing dishes with a simple wood brush, and opening a medicine cabinet with minimal supplies. Think about your motivation for ditching plastic waste and come back to it whenever you feel stuck.

**Know your trash.** Before you can start reducing waste, do a trash audit. Track what you're throwing away for one week and note any patterns. Just being aware of what you throw away each week will have a huge impact on your relationship to disposable products. You might notice the majority of your trash comes from packaged foods or beauty products. You might think twice before grabbing a plastic fork. You will also likely discover products that don't belong in the trash and can be recycled or composted instead.

**Use up disposables.** As tempting as it may be to toss all house-hold plastic and start fresh, I don't recommend it. For one, it's less wasteful to let each item serve its purpose before being thrown away. If you want to give your plastic bags and cutlery to someone who can use them, that works, too. Giving ourselves time to use up each disposable item helps us slow down and be thoughtful about how it will be replaced once it's gone, easing the transition to a waste-free lifestyle.

**Just say *no*.** One easy way to reduce waste is just to say *no* to single-use products such as plastic straws, cutlery, and bags. Assemble a kit to keep in your bag or car when you're on the go—a reusable tote, container, cutlery, cloth napkin, and Mason jar will help you avoid most trashy situations. If someone offers you free samples, swag, or party favors, ask yourself, "Is it worth the waste?"

**Go minimal.** Just going through the exercise of decluttering and taking a hard look at how many clothes, gadgets, and equipment we have can help reset wasteful habits. We become more mindful when making new purchases and are more likely to favor higher quality, reusable products over disposables. Also, having less stuff means less to store, clean, repair, and dispose of. Minimalism frees up time and space to care for the items we do value so they last longer and need to be replaced less often.

The US Environmental Protection Agency reports that, as of 2017, the average American produced 4.51 pounds of trash per day. The good news is, that's down from 4.74 pounds in 2000, but a significant jump compared to 2.68 pounds in 1960.

# The Plastic-Free(ish) Manifesto

There may be times when you feel stuck or discouraged on the road to a zero-waste lifestyle. Here are five mantras to help keep you going strong.

1. **Baby steps.** I recognize we're all impatient for results. We want to see our trash disappear—and we want it to disappear now! But, we're less likely to practice mindfulness and appreciate our progress when we race toward the finish line. Don't quit plastic cold turkey. Instead, give yourself time to research reusable alternatives, locate bulk options, and tinker with a DIY or two. Like any good habit, living zero waste can take more effort in the beginning and you might fumble before developing a rhythm. Slow down and enjoy the journey—it's a marathon, not a sprint.

2. **Progress not perfection.** You never know when a trashy situation might catch you by surprise. There may be days you forget to request no straw, or a plastic-wrapped sandwich is your only lunch option on the go. It can be easy to get caught up in eco-guilt and become discouraged when we're wasteful. It can be harder to appreciate all the progress made and ways we've succeeded. Remember, for the zero-waste movement to make a meaningful impact, we need a whole lot of people doing it imperfectly—not a handful of individuals fitting trash into a jar. Challenge yourself and set ambitious goals, but also forgive yourself if you're less than perfect.

3. **Hierarchy of needs.** As you go through this process, you will likely discover some items you can't find plastic free or aren't quite ready to part with. We have to balance zero waste with other competing needs, like time, ease, health, and income. There may be days when you're exhausted and don't have the energy to seek out the low-waste option. Or, you need a certain medication that only comes in plastic. Maybe it's a certain snack you love that comes in plastic and you don't want to make it yourself. There's no wrong way to reduce waste. If you're going to do zero waste for the long haul, do what works for you.

4. **Don't compare.** Set your goals and standards for success. You might look through Instagram or Pinterest (or even this book) and think, "*Why doesn't my home look like that?*" Remember, people tend to present the best version of themselves through social media, and it rarely shows the full picture—like how long it took them to get there and what missteps they made along the way. Rather than compare yourself to others, focus on your journey and progress. One person's path toward zero waste likely will look different from yours. Do the best you can with the resources available and try not to measure your progress by someone else's standards.

5. **Be the weirdo.** Doing things outside the norm may feel uncomfortable and intimidating at first. No one said being a zero-waste warrior was easy. Embrace your inner weirdo and don't apologize for caring about the environment. Yes, you might get some strange looks when you bring your reusable tumbler to a party or request take-out in your own reusable container, but you are doing your part to reduce waste and improve your lifestyle. You're also paving the way for others to step outside their comfort zone. People will be less timid about buying bulk foods in their own jar when they see other weirdos doing the same.

---

## ZERO WASTE: DOS AND DON'TS

✓ **Do** start with a trash audit. Think about whether each item you're about to toss is really trash, or can be recycled or composted instead.

✓ **Do** start composting food scraps and other organic waste.

✓ **Do** let friends, family, and coworkers know you are making a lifestyle change and offer concrete examples for how they can support you.

✗ **Don't** gather up all your plastic disposable products and throw them out at once—let each item serve its purpose before replacing it with something sustainable.

✗ **Don't** wishcycle items when you're unsure where they belong—brush up on local waste guidelines.

✗ **Don't** compare your progress to someone else's. Do the best you can with the resources available and make time to celebrate the wins (big and small).

# Plastic-Free(ish) Action Plan

Let's recap with some actionable steps to start reducing waste. Always make time to celebrate your achievements, whether big or small!

| SMALL WINS | BIG WINS |
| --- | --- |
| • Refuse plastic straws when you dine out and plastic bags when you shop. | • Bring your own container, cutlery and napkin so you can refuse disposables on the go. |
| • Reduce impulse spending by delaying a purchase for 24 hours. | • Reset shopping habits with a month-long spending freeze. |
| • Reuse an empty glass jar to store bulk food or freshly cut flowers. | • Repair, borrow or buy secondhand before purchasing something new. |
| • Recycle appropriate items—brush up on local guidelines so you don't wishcycle. | • Find collection sites for hard-to-recycle items like soft plastics and broken electronics. |
| • Rot food scraps and other organic materials through your municipal service or find a drop-off site. | • Start a home compost and use the nutrient-dense material to enrich your garden or houseplants. |

# KITCHEN

Our kitchen can say a lot about us. Just looking through someone's fridge or pantry offers insight into how we nourish and comfort ourselves, our dietary preferences and idiosyncrasies, and even our daily struggle for balance. We want to feel good about what we put into our bodies and how we feed our families, but sometimes, in the weekly chaos, just getting dinner on the table can be challenging. It's no wonder sustainability often takes a backseat.

Disposable products are so common in kitchens because they're cheap and convenient, helping us power through chores so we can get back to the things we actually enjoy. We have disposable plates and cutlery for entertaining and endless paper towels to wipe up life's messes. It's no surprise that the kitchen is where we generate the most waste.

When our family decided to ditch plastic, we knew focusing on our kitchen would make the biggest impact. We started by decluttering and parting with tools and gadgets that took up space and gathered dust. We gradually phased out single-use products and replaced them with reusable alternatives.

We were surprised to discover that living more minimally and switching to reusables made our lives easier and saved us time and money. It's less effort to use one cloth rag for cleaning than continuously tearing off paper towels—and we don't have to dash to the store to replace the empty roll. Taking care of our reusables requires more effort than throwing something away, but I've found unexpected joy in caring for these belongings and making them last. We're also more cautious with new purchases, and have been able to invest the money saved in good-quality tools we truly enjoy and value.

Five years in, we're still figuring out new ways to minimize plastic. It's unlikely you will ever achieve a *perfectly* plastic-free refrigerator, or pantry—but that isn't the goal. I'm not going to tell you to make your own crackers so you can skip packaged versions, or do without your favorite yogurt that comes in a plastic tub. Make plastic-free living work for you, savor your progress, and celebrate that with each small change you're making a positive impact on the environment, your health, and your family's well-being.

Ready to start? The easiest way to reduce kitchen waste is to prevent it from even entering your home. It's time to rethink the way we shop for groceries.

# Zero-Waste Grocery Kit

You may be in the habit of bringing reusable totes to the market; if so, you've already taken the first step toward zero-waste grocery shopping. With just a few additional tools, you can eliminate even more plastic from your shopping cart. Assembling your shopping kit is the easy part. Remembering to actually bring it to the store and working up the courage to use it can take time and practice, but soon it will become as routine as bringing a shopping list. Designate an area in your kitchen where you can quickly assemble a kit on your way out or stow it in your bag or car for impromptu trips to the store. I like to keep cloth produce bags and reusable totes folded in baskets in the same drawer so it's easy to remember both. I also customize my kit based on my shopping list—planning ahead and being prepared is key for plastic-free grocery shopping.

## THE ESSENTIALS

1. **Grocery list.** A list will help you estimate how many cloth bags and jars you'll need for your haul. Write it on a piece of scrap paper or keep it on your phone to go paperless.

2. **Reusable totes.** Look for tote bags with sturdy handles and a roomy base that can support heavy jars. You could also use a woven basket.

3. **Cloth produce bags.** Handy for purchasing small loose produce and dry bulk goods, without plastic bags. You can buy cloth bags online or DIY from scrap fabric.

4. **Mesh produce bags.** Mesh bags work best for loose produce such as oranges and brussels sprouts. The see-through material makes it easier for the cashier to identify your purchase without opening each bag.

5. **Glass jars with lids.** Depending on your list, you may want to bring a variety of sizes to buy wet items such as peanut butter and olives and fine dry goods such as flour and spices.

## THE EXTRAS

6. **Glass or stainless-steel container.** For purchasing meat, fish, and deli items, or grabbing a quick bite from the salad bar.

7. **Grease pencil (for jars) and washable marker or crayon (for cloth bags).** To mark the price look up (PLU) code for bulk items. Or, just track the codes on your phone.

groceries
✓ cheese
✓ apricots
✓ oats
✓ olives
✓ carrots
✓ chard

# Grocery Shopping

After completing your trash audit, you'll probably discover that food packaging makes up the majority of your household's waste. You might look at all this plastic and wonder if zero-waste groceries are even possible, but you'll be surprised how much waste you can avoid with a little preparation and the right supplies. You'll start to see your grocery store with fresh eyes and discover package-free goods everywhere you look. For example, most fresh produce already comes without packaging and items you'd typically buy in disposable bags or plastic tubs can often be purchased in bulk using your own bags or jars.

Learning to buy groceries without plastic does takes time, practice, and even a little *chutzpah*. We're creatures of habit trying to unlearn years (even decades) of wasteful habits and it might seem daunting or intimidating at first. It took me lots of online research and a few pep talks to work up the courage to buy peanut butter in my own jar. I was worried that people might think I was stealing, unhygienic, or a weird jar lady. What if I did it wrong and irritated the cashier or the other customers waiting in line? Luckily, the cashier was unfazed when I placed my jar on the conveyor belt. "I wish more people did this," she said, and continued ringing up my purchase.

Shopping in a new way feels foreign and people *might* give you the side eye, but it's usually because they're intrigued and want to know more. With practice, shopping without plastic will become second nature and you'll whip out your glass jars with confidence. My hope is that as zero waste goes mainstream, shopping without plastic will become the norm, not the other way around.

**Produce.** The beauty of avocados and bananas is they come packaged in a protective (and compostable) wrapper: their skin. Buying produce without plastic is easy: ditch the bag and place naked produce directly into your cart or basket. For damp greens like lettuce, or produce that sheds like broccoli, you might prefer

## BONUS POINTS

**Go ugly.** Reduce food waste by choosing "ugly" produce such as deformed carrots and lone bananas that would otherwise be tossed by the store.

**Go local.** Pay attention to labels that indicate where produce is grown—local options travel less distance to the store and, therefore, have a smaller carbon footprint.

**Go seasonal.** Give preference to produce that's in season where you live. Off-season produce is typically shipped from warmer climates and artificially ripened with chemicals that reduce flavor.

a cloth produce bag. Reusable bags are also handy for small loose items like mushrooms and brussels sprouts. Opt for spinach and whole heads of lettuce over pre-washed greens in plastic tubs and whole squash, zucchini, and carrots over the cubed, spiralized, or shredded versions that come in bags.

**Dairy.** Milk, cream, and yogurt can sometimes be found in refundable glass bottles and jars. You pay a deposit that's reimbursed when you return the empty bottle to the store. Wax paper butter wrappers can be composted and the cardboard box can be recycled. When butter is wrapped in foil, the packaging is often made from mixed materials and may not be recyclable. Cardboard egg cartons can also be recycled, composted, or reused to start seedlings for the garden. If your store has a cheese counter, get your wedge cut from a whole wheel, weighed, and placed in your container without plastic. Just watch the process—they may reach for plastic out of habit and need a *gentle* reminder.

**Meat.** Curbing your meat and dairy consumption is the single biggest way to reduce your environmental footprint. But, if you do eat meat, there are ways to lessen the environmental impact. Skip the packaged versions that come on plastic and foam trays and buy meat directly from the butcher in your own container. The butcher weighs the meat on a scale before filling your container and prints out a price sticker for you to take to the cashier. Also, don't be afraid to ask—the butcher always gets a big kick out of my husband bringing his own container and says he wished more people did the same. If you forget your container, ask the butcher to wrap your purchase in paper and compost it when you're done.

**Packaged goods.** Despite best efforts, purchasing some packaged foods may be unavoidable. If you can't find package-free versions of your essentials, buy the largest size available versus single servings such as chip bags or yogurt containers. Whenever possible, choose recyclable or compostable packaging such as glass, aluminum, and cardboard.

No receipt, please: When you're ready to check out, request paperless or no receipt—the paper is often coated with bisphenol A (BPA), a suspected carcinogen that can contaminate recycled paper products and harm your health. Always wash your hands after handling a receipt.

### OTHER GROCERIES

**Condiments.** Give preference to condiments packaged in glass or learn to make your own.

**Drinks.** Make your own beverages or give preference to drinks that come in glass bottles or aluminum cans.

**Frozen.** Skip it. The cardboard boxes are lined with plastic and typically are nonrecyclable.

# Bulk Foods

The bulk aisle is your new go-to destination for grains, beans, nuts, coffee, baking supplies, spices, snacks, and more. Buying in bulk not only eliminates packaging, but also reduces food waste and saves money because you can buy the exact amount you need. Trying a new recipe with an unfamiliar ingredient? Buy just what the recipe calls for; if it isn't a winner, you won't end up with a bag gathering dust in the pantry.

Bulk foods are also typically cheaper than packaged foods because you're not buying the branding and packaging built into the price. In terms of waste, most bulk aisles provide plastic bags to fill, but you can easily swap your own reusable cloth bags or jars (if the store's policy allows it). Cloth bags work best for large loose items like oats and trail mix; jars are useful for fine dry goods like flour and spices and wet goods like nut butter and honey.

## BEYOND THE BULK AISLE

**Bakery.** Fill up cloth bags with fresh bread, bagels, and rolls or bring a container for cakes, pies, tarts, and other sweet treats.

**Health and beauty.** Some stores offer bulk soap, shampoo, conditioner, and unpackaged bar soaps you can buy in your own jar or cloth bag.

**Olive bar.** From Kalamatas to Castelvetranos, marinated mushrooms to gigante beans and cornichons, the olive bar is a gold mine for package-free snacks and appetizers.

# Check Out My Zero-Waste Pantry

1.  **Keep it visible.** Storing pantry essentials on open shelves in glass jars makes it a cinch to see what you're running low on so you can add it to your grocery list.

2.  **Decant it.** Buy dry goods in bulk using cloth bags, then transfer into jars at home. For messy-to-decant items, like sugar and flour, bring jars to the store to fill directly.

3.  **When in doubt, label it.** Rice and pasta are easy to identify at a glance, but jars containing hard-to-identify items, like baking powder and flour, might benefit from a label.

4.  **Prevent pests.** Storing foods in airtight latch-top jars helps prevent spoiling and pest contamination.

5.  **Stock the staples.** Having staples such as grains, legumes, and nuts is handy for last-minute meals and snacks during a busy week.

6.  **Shop your pantry.** Plan meals around the items in your pantry to free up storage space and minimize food waste.

FLAKY SALT · BAKING POW· · KOSHER SAL· · BAKING SODA

# How to Buy in Bulk with a Jar

A glass jar is a versatile tool for bulk shopping, especially for wet items and fine dry goods like flour that can be messy to decant. Beyond the pantry, jars are useful for purchasing and storing bulk beauty and cleaning essentials like shampoo, dish soap, and powdered laundry detergent.

To start, you'll need to know the *tare*, or empty weight, of your container—usually in pounds if you live in the United States. When you're ready to pay, the cashier deducts the tare of the empty jar from the total weight of the filled jar to determine the price. The beauty of bringing your own container is you can buy as much or as little as you need and transfer it straight to your pantry (or shower or cleaning cupboard) at home.

**SUPPLIES**

Glass jar with lid

Kitchen scale

Paper tape and pen to label the tare, or grease pencil to write the tare directly on the jar

Policies allowing customers to fill their own containers can vary by store, city, and state based on local health and safety codes. It's best to call the store or check with the customer service desk before you fill up.

1. Place the lidded empty jar on a kitchen scale to determine its tare (weight).

2. Note the tare on the jar using a grease pencil, or label the jar with paper tape. Most stores in the United States will want the tare in pounds. For example, if your jar weighs 8 ounces, write the tare in pounds as 0.5 lbs. If your scale doesn't have a pounds-only unit, use an online conversion calculator.

3. Take the jar to the store and fill it with the bulk item.

4. Write the PLU (price look up) code on the jar, or track it on your phone (anywhere that's easily accessible).

5. Dictate the PLU to the cashier if it's not labeled on the jar.

6. Transfer the jar to your pantry or refrigerator at home. If the item in the jar is not easily identifiable, label it so you don't forget.

**TIP** No scale? No problem. Bring your jar to the customer service desk or deli counter. They can use their scale to weigh and label the jar for you.

# BULK SHOPPING WITH JARS: DOS AND DON'TS

✓ **Do** call ahead or stop by the customer service desk to confirm your store's jar refill policy.

✓ **Do** repurpose empty pasta sauce, pickle, and jam jars (cleaned, with labels removed).

✓ **Do** consider the neck size of your bottle or jar—a wide mouth makes spills less likely when you're filling up.

✗ **Don't** forget to label the tare and PLU code, or track them on your phone. The cashier and customers in line behind you will appreciate you being prepared.

✗ **Don't** bring jars that haven't been thoroughly washed and dried. It can violate health and safety codes and may cause your store to reverse its policy (*not* cool).

✗ **Don't** load up on bulky jars if you're biking, walking, or wrangling a toddler. A couple of small jars or lightweight cloth produce bags will give your back a break.

# Where to Find Bulk

Food co-ops and health food stores are great resources for bulk foods as well as beauty and cleaning supplies. If your regular grocery store doesn't have a bulk aisle, or doesn't offer the items you need, there are other creative ways to find package-free goods. Look for small local businesses, such as the ones listed below, for a range of bulk options. It's a great way to support your community and smaller shops are often more willing to accommodate special requests, like filling your own containers—some even offer a discount!

## SECRET(ISH) BULK OPTIONS

Asian markets for herbs, produce, tea, and tofu

Bakeries for bread, cookies, pastries, and rolls

Breweries for beer refills

Butcher shops for meat, bones, and stock

Cheese shops for fresh-cut cheese from the wheel

Coffee roasters for bulk coffee beans

Delis for sliced cheeses, meats, and prepared salads

Ice-cream parlors and gelaterias for frozen treats

Indian markets for legumes, rice, and spices

Italian markets for fresh cheeses, pasta, sauces, and olives

Mexican groceries for chips, dried chili peppers, and tortillas

Middle Eastern markets for dolmas, falafel, hummus, and pita

Spice stores for trying new flavors in small quantities

Sweet shops for bulk candy and chocolate

Tea shops for loose-leaf tea

Wineries for local wines

# Walnut Butter

As a vegetarian who eats limited dairy, nut butter has become an essential source of protein and a pantry staple in my home. I like to slather it on rice cakes and toast, bake it into bars and cookies, swirl it into oats and yogurt, and, of course, eat it directly from the jar with a spoon. With a jar-a-week habit, finding a way to make it zero waste was a game changer.

I started by buying fresh-grind peanut butter and almond butter in the bulk section, which was delicious—but pricey. I began to wonder how hard it would be to make my own. I started blending various nuts I bought in bulk and was surprised to discover it was actually pretty easy. My absolute favorite is walnut butter, which is full of omega-3 fatty acids and has a rich, satisfying flavor that can elevate even the blandest bread. You can add optional sweeteners and spices, like honey, maple syrup, or cinnamon, but be sure to mix them in after you're done blending.

## MAKES ABOUT 2 CUPS

### INGREDIENTS

4 cups raw walnuts

### SUPPLIES

1 baking sheet

High-speed blender

Glass storage jar
(16 ounce)

1. Preheat the oven to 350°F.

2. Spread the walnuts in an even layer on a baking sheet. Bake until golden and fragrant, 10 to 12 minutes.

3. Remove from the oven and let cool for 10 minutes. Transfer the walnuts to a high-speed blender and blend on low speed, using the tamper wand to push the walnuts toward the blade. If you don't have a tamper and the grinding seems sluggish, turn off the machine every few minutes and loosen the walnuts with a spatula, scraping down the sides of the blender.

4. The texture will be crumbly at first. Keep pushing the nuts toward the blade with the tamper or spatula until it becomes smooth, or reaches your desired consistency. It takes me about 10 minutes to get a smooth, creamy butter.

5. Store the nut butter in a jar with an airtight seal in the pantry for up to three weeks, or refrigerate for 6 to 8 months.

**TIP** You can also make nut butter in a food processor. Scrape down the sides as needed to get it to a smooth consistency.

# Beverages

**Coffee.** Single-use coffee pods are super convenient and super wasteful. A low-waste coffee routine starts by purchasing whole or ground beans from the bulk section at the market or your favorite local roaster. To make your brew, try a French press, stovetop espresso maker, pour over with a reusable cloth filter, or even a reusable pod for your Keurig or Nespresso machine. Compost used grounds, repurpose them as body scrub, or mix them into garden soil as a natural fertilizer and pesticide—they're great for acid-loving plants like hydrangeas.

**Tea.** There's nothing like a nice hot cup of plastic—*amiright*? Many tea bags, especially those pyramid-shaped "silky" ones, are made from plastic or come packaged in paper sleeves with a plastic lining. Loose-leaf tea is more flavorful than tea bags and can be bought in bulk at the market or a specialty tea shop in your own jar. For hot water, use a stovetop or electric kettle, but try to select one with minimal plastic on the interior, especially parts that come into contact with the water—heat causes the plastic to leach chemicals. To steep the leaves, try a loose-leaf teapot or a stainless-steel tea infuser for a single cup.

**Water.** One word: *microplastics*. Did you know bottled water is less regulated for water quality compared to tap, and is filled with tiny plastic particles? If you don't like the taste of tap water, invest in a water filter for your faucet or a glass pitcher with a built-in filter (most manufacturers offer take-back programs to recycle filters). Many people also swear by charcoal sticks—a natural water purifier that you place in a pitcher of water to remove impurities like chlorine and pesticides—but note they take much longer to work compared to a built-in filter (two to three hours until the water is ready to drink). If you prefer cold water, fill a glass carafe and place it in the fridge, or add ice from a stainless-steel or silicone ice tray.

# Farmers' Markets

The farmers' market is a great way to connect with your food supply and support local farms. Buying local also helps minimize the distance food travels to your plate—an average of 1,500 miles in the United States. Unlike industrial farms, local farms produce smaller food quantities to meet community demand. They also tend to favor organic growing practices that help protect the local habitat and reduce exposure to pesticides. Here are a few more reasons to shop at the farmers' market.

**Taste the difference.** Have you ever wondered why a freshly picked tomato tastes so much better than store bought? Produce at grocery stores is often harvested early so it can be shipped and distributed over long distances and ripen along the way. It's also covered in pesticides, waxes, and preservatives to maintain a fresh appearance, and chilled to prevent spoiling—all of which reduces flavor. By contrast, produce at the farmers' market is grown within a few miles of where you live and ripens naturally in the field, maximizing freshness and flavor.

**Skip unnecessary packaging.** It's easier to avoid unnecessary packaging at the farmers' market, like those annoying plastic produce stickers on apples and pears at the grocery store. If you're buying berries, ask the vendor whether they can reuse the plastic or cardboard basket they come in, then empty the contents into your own container. Same with rubber bands and twist ties. If you see something you'd like to buy that comes in packaging, like homemade tortillas or cheese, ask whether the vendor would be willing to bring it the following week sans plastic. It never hurts to ask, and if enough people request plastic-free options, they'll be more incentivized to switch to something sustainable.

**Practice BYOC (bring your own container).** In addition to fresh produce, many markets have an assortment of food stands and coffee trucks—making it an ideal place to practice asking for food and beverages in your own containers. We love going to our market on Sunday morning, grabbing a latte in a reusable mug and dim sum or tamales in a stainless-steel container for breakfast. People in line are often curious about our containers and, hopefully, we've made it less scary for others to bring their own when eating at the market. By asking for food in a reusable container, you help pave the way for others in your community to do the same.

A local farmers' market is a luxury not everyone can access. If you don't have one close by, look into a community-supported agriculture (CSA) box by which local farms deliver fruits, vegetables, and occasionally eggs, meat, and honey to your home. Or, join a community garden or neighbor crop swap, or start your own!

# Food Storage and Preparation

We can all help protect the environment by being more mindful about the foods we buy and how we buy them. And, we can protect our health by being thoughtful about how we store and prepare foods and beverages. Studies have shown that plastic leaches toxic chemicals into our food and drink, which can mess with our hormones. (I don't know about you, but my hormones don't need additional stress.)

If you need another reason, plastic is an eyesore and trains us to treat our belongings as though they're disposable. When we invest in products that last, made from natural materials, we become more conscious consumers and take better care of our purchases. They can even add beauty to mundane chores, like washing dishes, and make them a little more joyful (*really*).

# Check Out My Zero-Waste Fridge

1. **Make a fruit basket.** Place fruit in a basket or bowl at eye level so it is more likely to be seen and consumed.

2. **FIFO.** Practicing the first-in, first-out rule, place older and perishable foods like yogurt and leftovers toward the front so they're less likely to be forgotten.

3. **Line your drawers.** Keep refrigerator crisper drawers tidy by lining them with folded tea towels. Then, add loose fruits and vegetables for plastic-free storage.

4. **Stick it in water.** Keep asparagus and carrots crisp by placing them in a jar of water. For more food storage tips, turn to page 48.

5. **Keep it clear.** Storing foods in transparent glass containers makes it easier to see what you have at a glance.

6. **Hydrate greens.** Store delicate greens and herbs, like lettuce, dill, and cilantro, in a cotton produce storage bag. The bag keeps produce hydrated and crisp while wicking away excess moisture.

7. **Organize by theme.** To keep your food tidy and accessible, organize sections by theme. The top shelf is mostly breakfast items, the middle shelf is leftovers and snacks, and the bottom shelf and crisper are for whole and partially-used produce.

8. **Wrap it up.** Preserve half a melon or avocado with a beeswax cloth wrap instead of plastic wrap or a disposable bag.

# Food Storage

**Jars and containers.** Glass jars are the workhorses of a zero-waste kitchen. They can be used to buy food in bulk, store pantry essentials, and transport meals on the go. Glass jars can also be used to freeze leftover sauces and soups, but be sure to leave an inch or two of empty space at the top to allow for expansion so the jars don't crack. Latch-top jars, like those made by Le Parfait or Bormioli Rocco, are airtight and easy to fill and look more organized in your pantry than a jumble of plastic bags. It's also good to have a set of glass storage containers. Most come with plastic or rubber lids, but there are now options made from bamboo, stainless steel, and even glass.

**Produce bags.** Believe it or not, produce can be kept fresh without plastic bags. If you've ever discovered a bag of slimy greens in the fridge, you know it's a depressing sight. It turns out delicate greens such as lettuce, arugula, and fresh herbs prefer being stored in breathable cotton and thrive in a humid environment. A damp cotton storage bag or tea towel hydrates greens while wicking away moisture and keeps them crisp for weeks—preventing food waste and saving money. I like to keep a water-filled spray bottle in the kitchen to give greens and herbs a quick spritz before they go into the bag, and every few days afterward if they start to dry out.

**Sandwich bags and food wrap.** If you want to keep things light, especially for school lunches and travel, use reusable silicone bags to pack snacks and sandwiches and ditch the plastic waste. You can even write your kid's name or a special note on the bags with a chalk pen. Instead of plastic cling wrap, try beeswax cloths to preserve half an avocado or wedge of cheese, or use it to cover a bowl of leftovers. The warmth from your fingertips easily shapes and seals the cloth, and unlike plastic wrap, it can be washed and reused again and again. Many last up to a year and can be composted at the end of their useful life (and they smell like honey, *yum*). There are also vegan versions made from candelilla wax.

# Guide for Storing Fruits and Vegetables

For many people, grocery shopping happens once, maybe twice, a week and the time between buying and consuming purchases can stretch for days and sometimes weeks. Before I went zero waste, I thought plastic was the only way to keep foods fresh at home. But, as I started eliminating plastic from grocery trips, I discovered more sustainable ways to maintain freshness and prevent food waste. Here are some simple guidelines for storing produce without plastic.

- **Apples:** Refrigerate loose in a bowl or the crisper.

- **Arugula:** Refrigerate in a damp cloth bag or towel and place in the crisper.

- **Asparagus:** Trim woody ends and refrigerate stalks in a jar of water.

- **Avocado:** Store on the counter until ripe, then refrigerate.

- **Bananas:** Store on the counter, away from ethylene-sensitive produce like apples and potatoes.

- **Basil:** Trim the stem ends and store in a jar of water on the counter. The stems will sprout roots after a few days, and you can even transplant them into your garden.

- **Beets:** Separate the greens from the roots. Refrigerate the roots loose in the crisper and the greens in a damp cloth bag or towel (they're great in a smoothie or stir-fry).

- **Bell peppers:** Refrigerate loose in the crisper.

- **Berries:** Refrigerate in a glass container; don't wash until you're ready to use them.

- **Bok choy:** Refrigerate in a damp cloth bag or towel in the crisper.

- **Broccoli:** Refrigerate loose in the crisper.

- **Brussels sprouts:** Refrigerate in a cloth bag or loose in the crisper.

- **Cabbage:** Refrigerate loose in the crisper.

- **Carrots:** Separate the greens from the roots. Refrigerate carrots in an airtight container or in a jar of water with the roots pointed down. Greens can be composted or repurposed into pesto.

- **Cauliflower:** Refrigerate in the crisper.

- **Celery:** Refrigerate loose in the crisper.

- **Chard:** Refrigerate in a damp cloth bag or towel in the crisper.

- **Citrus:** Refrigerate loose in the crisper, or a bowl.

- **Corn:** Refrigerate, in its husk, loose in the crisper.

- **Cucumber:** Refrigerate loose in the crisper.

- **Eggplant:** Refrigerate loose in the crisper.

- **Figs:** Refrigerate in a single layer on a plate.

- **Garlic:** Store on the counter.

- **Grapes:** Refrigerate in a cloth bag in the crisper, or loose in a bowl.

- **Green beans:** Refrigerate in a damp cloth bag or towel in the crisper.

- **Herbs (except basil):** Refrigerate in a damp cloth bag or towel in the crisper.

- **Kiwi:** Store on the counter until ripe, then place in the crisper.

- **Leeks:** Wrap in a damp cloth bag or towel and place in the crisper. Stalks can be trimmed and saved for stock.

- **Lettuce:** Refrigerate whole heads in a damp cloth bag or towel. Chopped or loose-leaf lettuces can be refrigerated in a glass container.

- **Melon:** Store on the counter until ripe, then refrigerate.

- **Mushrooms:** Refrigerate in a glass container.

- **Onions:** Store on the counter.

- **Pears:** Store on the counter until ripe, then refrigerate.

- **Persimmons:** Store on the counter until ripe, then refrigerate.

- **Pineapple:** Store on the counter until ripe—when you can easily pull out a leaf. Then, eat immediately or cut into slices and refrigerate in a container.

- **Pomegranate:** Store on the counter or remove the seeds (arils) and refrigerate them in a jar.

- **Potatoes:** Store in a dark drawer or cupboard.

- **Radishes:** Separate the greens from the roots. Rinse the radishes and refrigerate in a jar of water. Change the water every few days. The greens can be eaten raw in a salad or turned into pesto.

- **Scallions:** Place in a jar of water and keep on the counter.

- **Spinach:** Wrap in a damp cloth bag or towel and place in the crisper.

- **Stone fruit:** Store on the counter until ripe, then transfer to the crisper.

- **Tomatoes:** Store on the counter.

- **Zucchini:** Refrigerate loose in the crisper.

### OTHER GROCERIES

**Bread.** Unlike packaged sliced bread, fresh bread goes stale six times faster in the refrigerator versus at room temperature. To maintain freshness, keep the loaf whole and store it in a bread box or breathable cloth bag on the counter. Most bread should be consumed within two to three days and baguettes within 24 hours. For longer storage, slice and freeze bread in a cloth bag or glass container.

**Cheese.** Wrapping cheese in plastic prevents it from breathing and reduces its flavor. Refrigerate soft cheese in a glass container. Wrap hard cheese in reusable beeswax cloth or compostable parchment paper before placing it in a container in the refrigerator.

# 5 Ways to Reduce Food Waste

You might be surprised to learn that plastic is *not* the most wasted material in landfills; it's food (plastic is second). Food waste is a huge problem in the United States. The National Resources Defense Council estimates a family of four throws away more than $1,800 worth of groceries each year. Before I went zero waste, I often felt as though I had a fridge full of food, yet nothing to eat. I took my privilege to buy whatever groceries I desired for granted, but I felt guilty whenever I found a bag of rotten produce in the crisper drawer.

A mental shift occurs when you switch to a zero-waste lifestyle. I started treating my belongings with more care—including food. Challenging myself to waste less food has helped me become a more creative cook, and I feel satisfaction as my refrigerator becomes emptier as the week hums along. An emptier fridge also makes it easier to clean and tidy between grocery trips.

We've reviewed how to store produce and other food items properly to reduce food waste. Here are a few additional ideas to consider.

1. **Have a plan.** Making a daily meal plan before you shop helps simplify dinners during a busy week and makes it more likely you'll use the groceries you buy. I like to plan meals that can be customized by what's in season, and mixed and matched. For example, roasted vegetables can be added to a rice bowl, be tossed in pasta, or top polenta.

2. **Stick with basics.** How many times have you planned to try healthy or trendy new recipes but ordered take-out instead? Trying new recipes is a great way to add variety to your rotation, but consider a limit of once or twice per week. You are more likely to cook what's in your fridge when you have easy-to-make staples you can prepare on autopilot.

3. **Shop your fridge and pantry.** Taking an inventory of your fridge and pantry before you shop makes it easier to plan meals around the foods you have, especially perishable produce, and reduce food waste. I discovered one of my favorite recipes trying to find a way to use up leftover wild rice.

4. **FIFO rule.** Using the first-in, first-out rule, place older foods toward the front of your refrigerator so you are more likely to use them. I do this with leftovers and cut-up produce, keeping them eye level on the middle shelf. Also, storing food in transparent glass makes it easier to see what you have so nothing gets forgotten.

5. **Think like a chef.** A good chef can find creative ways to use everything so no food goes to waste. They save vegetable scraps and animal bones for stocks, blitz leftover greens and nuts into savory pesto, extract both the juice and zest from citrus for vinaigrettes and cakes, and transform stale bread into bread crumbs and croutons. For example, I discovered broccoli stalks are delicious when they are peeled and roasted with olive oil, salt, and pepper.

# Vegetable Scrap Stock

Making your own vegetable stock is surprisingly easy, and a great way to reuse scraps and peels. And, once you taste homemade stock, you'll never want to return to the packaged stuff. Stock is an essential component for soups and stews, but can also pack flavor into risottos, quinoa, curries, and sauces. You can refrigerate it for up to one week, or freeze it in a few jars for up to three months.

MAKES 8 TO 10 CUPS

### INGREDIENTS

4 cups vegetable scraps (see Tip)

2 carrots, roughly chopped

2 celery stalks, roughly chopped

1 onion, roughly chopped

2 bay leaves

### SUPPLIES

1 large pot

1 fine-mesh sieve

1 large heatproof bowl

1 slotted spoon or tongs

2–3 glass storage jars (1 quart) with lids

1. In a large soup pot or Dutch oven, combine the scraps, carrots, celery, onion, and bay leaves. Add 10 to 12 cups water, enough to cover the vegetables by 1 to 2 inches.

2. Bring the mixture to a boil over high heat, then lower the heat and simmer, uncovered, for 1 hour, occasionally stirring.

3. Turn off the heat. Strain the stock through a fine-mesh sieve set over a large heatproof bowl. Let the solids cool a bit, then squeeze them with your hands, or use the back of a spoon to extract any remaining liquid. Compost the solids.

4. Let the stock cool to room temperature, then refrigerate in 2 or 3 one-quart glass jars. Or, use several smaller jars or an ice tray to freeze it in smaller portions. If freezing, be sure to leave 1 to 2 inches at the top of the jar to allow for expansion so your jars don't break.

**TIP** Vegetable scraps can include roots, stalks, leaves, and peels from bell pepper, carrot, celery, corncobs, eggplant, fennel, garlic, green beans, herbs, leek, mushrooms, onion, parsnip, peas, potato, scallion, shallot, tomato, and winter squash. *Avoid* artichokes, broccoli, brussels sprouts, cabbage, cauliflower, and turnips, which can make your stock bitter.

# Cooking and Dining

Our kitchens have become a catchall for gadgets and gizmos that seem like a good idea, in theory. Popcorn makers, air fryers, and sous vide gear that promise to make cooking easier, more flavorful—and don't forget fun. These tools take up space, clutter drawers and cabinets, and trap us in an endless cycle of buying the next best thing. Like too much food in the fridge, a surplus of cooking tools makes it harder to clean and organize and more likely to forget what we already have and purchase a duplicate.

Take reusable totes—stores love to give away their branded bags, and we take them because they're "eco-friendly!" Soon, we end up with a dozen reusable totes taking up an entire kitchen cupboard (probably a low estimate). When we minimize to the essentials, our kitchens become more spacious and productive, we take better care of our belongings, and we are more cautious about new purchases.

Although I recommend a gradual approach to phasing plastic out of the home, cookware might be the exception. When plastic and nonstick surfaces, like Teflon, are exposed to heat, they leach chemicals into our food, many of which are suspected carcinogens. It's best to stick to cookware made from cast iron, stainless steel, glass, and wood. If you need to replace essentials, shop for them secondhand at thrift stores, garage sales, and buy-sell-trade groups online. If you can't find something secondhand, restaurant supply stores are a great resource for long-lasting, quality kitchen tools at an affordable price. Here are some of my recommended essentials (and a few extras) for the kitchen.

## PREP

Colander (enamel or stainless steel)

Cooking spoon (wood)

Cutting board (wood)

Grater

Kitchen shears

Knife sharpener

Knives (chef's, paring, and serrated)

Pepper grinder

Saltcellar

Sieve, fine-mesh (stainless steel)

Slotted spoon (enamel, stainless steel, or wood)

Spatulas (silicone and stainless steel)

Tongs (stainless steel)

Vegetable peeler

Whisk (stainless steel)

## COOKWARE

Dutch oven, or large stainless-steel pot

Saucepan (stainless steel)

Skillet (cast iron or stainless steel)

## BAKING

2 baking sheets

2 or 3 mixing bowls (ceramic, glass, or stainless steel)

1 pair of oven mitts (or use folded towels)

Glass measuring cup for liquids

Measuring cups for baking (ceramic, enamel, or stainless steel)

Measuring spoons (ceramic, enamel, or stainless steel)

## STORAGE

Beeswax cloths (optional)

Cloth bowl covers (optional)

Glass jars with lids (canning or latch top)

Glass storage containers with lids (range of sizes)

Silicone bags (optional)

## DINING (IN MULTIPLES OF EIGHT OR MORE, DEPENDING ON YOUR FAMILY'S SIZE)

Bowls

Cutlery

Dinner plates

Glass tumblers

Napkins (cotton or linen)

Salad plates

Wineglasses or tumblers

Our cast-iron skillet is our most used pan—from omelets to pizzas to giant cookie cakes (*nom, nom*). Remember to use only water to clean it; *never* soap—it can ruin the pan's seasoning, which makes it naturally nonstick.

## CLEANING

Cloth rags (cotton or bamboo)

Dish brush (wood)

Scrubber (copper)

4 tea towels (cotton, linen, hemp, or bamboo)

## THE EXTRAS

A few of the extras we love at home (take 'em or leave 'em):

**Glass juicer.** Works ten times better than those handheld citrus squeezers (IMO), but a fork and firm grip will also work.

**High-speed blender.** The one appliance I can't do without—for everything from smoothies to soups to nut butters and pasta sauce.

**Kitchen scale.** A favorite tool for precise measuring when baking and taring jars for bulk grocery shopping (*of course*).

**Silicone baking mats.** These reusable mats fit standard baking sheets and replace parchment paper. Use for everything from roasting vegetables to baking cookies.

**Stainless-steel salad spinner.** Our family is more likely to eat greens if they're washed and ready to go. You could also wash leaves over your sink and pat dry with towels.

## WHEN YOU FEEL LIKE COOKING . . .

Switching from prepared foods to raw ingredients bought in bulk requires some preparation and cooking. Making things from scratch can provide a sense of empowerment and reassurance that we are consuming whole ingredients and nothing else—and, the more we cook, the more connected we are to what we eat. Zero waste doesn't mean you have to turn into Martha Stewart overnight and make everything from scratch, and you might not have the time or desire to do so. Start slowly, trying basics like stovetop beans, or my favorite simple recipes for Vegetable Scrap Stock (page 52), and Kitchen Sink Granola (page 171).

## WHEN YOU FEEL LIKE TAKE-OUT . . .

To make zero waste work over the long run, there has to be a balance between sustainability and ease. Just because you go plastic free doesn't mean you can't enjoy take-out from your favorite restaurant every now and then. Start by requesting no extras, like plastic utensils or sauce packets. For pick up, bring a reusable cloth bag or skip the bag altogether and carry out your meal by hand. When you work up the courage, ask the restaurant to fill your reusable container. And don't forget to bring a container for leftovers when you dine out—paper take-out boxes are often lined with plastic, making them non-recyclable and non-compostable.

## You Can Compost That

In addition to food scraps, did you know you can compost . . .

- Coffee grounds and filters
- Cupcake and muffin wrappers*
- Donut and pastry boxes*
- Paper bags
- Paper napkins and paper towels
- Paper plates
- Pastry bags*
- Pizza boxes
- Tea bags (be sure to remove the staple)*
- Toothpicks
- Wax paper butter wrappers
- Wood skewers

\* Made from paper only

# Plastic-Free(ish) Action Plan

|  |  |
|---|---|
| **SMALL WINS** | **BIG WINS** |
| • Skip plastic bags and buy naked produce. | • Shop for produce and bulk foods with cloth bags and jars. |
| • Buy the largest package size of snacks to avoid single-use servings. | • Buy snacks or ingredients to make your own from the bulk section. |
| • Switch from bottled water to tap water with a filter, if local water quality meets public safety standards. | • Swap single-use coffee pods and tea bags for bulk beans or grounds and loose-leaf tea. |
| • Compost food scraps (see page 194 for compost methods). | • Repurpose food scraps for stocks, garnishes, and baking. |
| • Request no disposables when you order take-out. | • Request take-out in your reusable containers. |

While the kitchen produces the most waste at home, the bathroom presents a different set of obstacles to plastic-free living. For one, we've been led to believe we need hundreds of different products to be sanitary, healthy, and beautiful, many of which are designed to be tossed after a single use. For another, it can be hard to find plastic-free alternatives for many bathroom essentials, let alone ones you actually like. Many years ago when I started going zero waste, it seemed as though the only option was to make my own lotion, toothpaste, and mascara (when I was feeling brave).

While I enjoy the modest DIY now and then, early attempts had me schlepping all over the Bay Area to track down ingredients—some of which came in plastic packaging. After a particularly disastrous lotion experiment, I realized I didn't have the patience for DIYs with more than three ingredients that could easily be found at my local grocery store.

Lucky for me (and you), plastic-free beauty products have taken off in the last few years, from package-free shampoo bars to metal tubes of toothpaste to body wash in refillable glass bottles. Sustainable options are popping up everywhere thanks to the momentum of the plastic-free movement and growing consumer demand for earth-friendly solutions. Even mainstream brands are joining the bandwagon—Pantene, The Body Shop, and Gillette are piloting refillable, recyclable packaging with Loop, a milkman-style delivery service.

But, before you buy a bunch of new health and beauty products, start with a bathroom audit—take stock of everything you've stowed in the shower, vanity, and medicine cabinet. You'll likely discover products that serve the same purpose, expired items, and things you've held onto out of guilt like the wrong shade of expensive lipstick. Streamlining your products will help simplify your routine, reduce waste, and give you more bandwidth to integrate plastic-free alternatives.

We all have different health and beauty priorities and deciding what you put onto and into your body is such a personal choice. What works for one person's skin and hair might be a hot mess for someone else, and there may be times you decide to stick with the plastic-y product. Focus on the big picture and don't beat yourself up if you still produce a little waste in your beauty routine.

# Zero-Waste Bathroom Kit

There are many ways to reduce plastic waste in the bathroom. It starts with simplifying your routine and using up what you already have. When you're ready to replace single-use products, the plastic-free options are, pretty much, endless. You have to find what works for you, whether you switch to a shampoo bar or purchase your favorite brand in bulk. Here are a few reusable tools to get you started.

## THE ESSENTIALS

1. **Bamboo toothbrush.** Stop sending plastic toothbrushes to landfill and switch to a compostable bamboo toothbrush. Be sure to remove the nylon bristles before you compost the handle.

2. **Deodorant.** Swap plastic deodorant sticks for a natural deodorant in a cardboard tube or glass jar. You can smell fresh, protect your health, *and* protect the planet all at the same time.

3. **Menstrual cup.** Your new best friend during *that* time of month. You could also try reusable menstrual pads or period panties.

4. **Reusable facial rounds.** Ditch single-use cotton balls and makeup remover wipes with reusable facial rounds. Cleanse your face, apply toner, and toss them in the wash.

5. **Safety razor.** Switch from disposable razors to a reusable safety razor. It will last a lifetime and the blades can be recycled.

6. **Silk floss.** Protect your gums and marine animals by switching to compostable silk dental floss. It comes in a glass vial that can be refilled when you run out.

7. **Variety of glass bottles and jars.** Fill with bulk or DIY shampoo, conditioner, body wash, makeup remover, and lotion.

## THE EXTRAS

8. **Compostable cotton swabs.** (Not pictured.) Ditch plastic cotton swabs for a compostable version made from cardboard and cotton, or try a reusable silicone "cotton" swab.

9. **Plastic-free toothpaste.** If making your own toothpaste isn't appealing, buy a toothpaste that comes in a glass jar or metal tube and recycle the empty container.

10. **Toilet paper.** Look for recycled TP sold in a cardboard box with individual rolls wrapped in paper. Or, take it a step further and switch to a bidet and cloth toilet unpaper.

11. **Wood bath brush.** Skip the plastic loofah and exfoliate your skin with a wood bath brush with natural bristles. You could also use a washcloth or natural loofah.

12. **Wood hairbrush.** When your plastic hairbrush is no longer usable, switch to a long-lasting wood brush that can be composted at the end of its useful life.

# Check Out My Zero-Waste Bathroom Vanity

1. **Think recycled.** Swap plastic-wrapped TP for a paper-wrapped version. This one is made from recycled schoolbooks by Who Gives a Crap.

2. **Think repurposed.** Corral loose objects with repurposed containers and baskets found around your home. These reusable cotton facial rounds are stored in a glass Weck jar.

3. **Think compostable.** A wood facial cleansing brush and nailbrush are not only beautiful, but can also be composted at the end of their useful life.

4. **Think minimal.** Streamlining products to those used daily helps keep drawers tidy and organized.

5. **Think packaging.** Favor health and beauty products that come in recyclable or compostable (or reusable!) packaging. These Fat and the Moon cosmetics come in metal tins.

6. **Think tidy.** Keeping a stack of cloth rags and All-Purpose Cleaner (page 97) handy makes it easier to tidy up.

# Skin Care and Makeup

Skin is our largest organ and our first line of defense from temperature extremes, injuries, and toxic chemicals. We're pretty good at questioning unfamiliar ingredients found in our food and beverages, but what about health and beauty products? Our skin absorbs all the lotions, serums, and soaps we apply to it daily, and the scary thing is, many of these products contain chemicals that aren't regulated.

It can be hard to know which products to trust—even ones marketed as *natural* may contain harmful ingredients you wouldn't want anywhere near your body. But, even if we do find an organic product with ingredients so pure you could eat it, they're often packaged in wasteful plastic tubes and bottles that end up in landfill. There can be a disconnect between products that are good for your health but that come in packaging that is bad for the environment. You may have to experiment with different products and go through some trial and error before you find the right solution for your skin.

**Face scrubs.** Did you know many exfoliants, and even some toothpastes, contain microbeads (small plastic particles, so tiny they sneak past wastewater treatment plants and end up in the ocean)? Although lots of countries—including the United States, Canada, and many European countries—have banned the manufacture of products that contain microbeads, the interpretation of these bans varies. Check your exfoliant to make sure it doesn't contain plastic microbeads made from polyethylene, polypropylene, or nylon. Products with natural exfoliants, like ground walnut shells and apricot pits, are a good alternative, or make your own exfoliating scrub from sugar, ground oats, salt, baking soda, or coffee grounds (bonus points for reusing grounds from your morning brew).

**Lotion.** There are tons of options for plastic-free lotion. You can find it in a refillable and recyclable aluminum bottle from Plaine Products and in a glass jar from Fat and the Moon. There are even solid lotion bars—the warmth of your hands helps soften the bar so you can easily apply the lotion to your body. There are also many DIY lotions online, or if you want to keep things simple, coconut oil, jojoba seed oil, rosehip oil, sweet almond oil, and olive oil all make great natural moisturizers and can, sometimes, be found available for purchase in bulk.

**Makeup.** Just because you're reducing waste doesn't mean you have to go makeup free. There are a lot of zero-waste makeup options entering the market, many sold in cardboard, metal, or glass packaging, such as from RMS Beauty, Elate Cosmetics, ILIA Beauty, and Kjaer Weis. Finding plastic-free makeup that works for your complexion can take some experimenting—I tried six different mascaras before I found one that worked well and didn't give me raccoon eyes (Elate mascara was the winner).

Some brands offer take-back recycling programs. M•A•C Cosmetics rewards customers with a free lipstick for every six empty M•A•C products returned to their store and Origins offers an in-store recycling program regardless of brand.

**Soap.** Plastic-free face and body soap is easy to find. Bar soap is a timeless solution that comes wrapped in paper, in a cardboard box, or loose without packaging. Options can be found at health food stores and some farmers' markets (buying local is always a plus). If you can't find local brands, there are great options online—some of my favorites are the Chagrin Valley Soap & Salve Company and Meow Meow Tweet. If you prefer liquid soap, you can sometimes find it in bulk and fill your own jar. Many people swear by Castile soap, like Dr. Bronner's, which can be used to wash hands, hair, dishes, and even clothing. For additional refill options, look into Plaine Products, whose products are sold in aluminum bottles, and Bathing Culture, whose products are sold in glass.

**Sunscreen.** You don't have to hide under an umbrella for zero-waste sun protection (though, it couldn't hurt). Plastic-free sunscreen can be found in glass jars, bottles, and, my personal favorite, a recyclable metal tin from Raw Elements. No matter which option you choose, check to make sure it's reef safe—some common ingredients, oxybenzone and octinoxate, not only bleach coral reefs, they may also be harmful to our health. These two ingredients are so destructive to the ocean environment that Hawaii banned the sale of products containing either chemical in 2018.

If you have a beauty brand you love and aren't ready to part with, contact the manufacturer—the more customers who ask for plastic-free packaging, the more likely the company will offer it.

# Check Out My Zero-Waste Makeup Bag

1. My favorite Elate **mascara** comes encased in a compostable bamboo tube and can be refilled.

2. Products like this Fat and the Moon **lip and cheek stain** and **lip salve** are packaged in metal tins that are reusable and recyclable.

3. Look for **compostable cotton swabs** made from cotton and bamboo or cardboard.

4. Try **reusable cotton facial rounds** for removing makeup and applying toner.

5. This **primer** comes in a glass jar that can be recycled at M•A•C Cosmetics.

6. This Baggu **dopp kit** is made from recycled heavyweight nylon.

# Makeup Remover

I have a hard time not touching my face, and at the end of a long day, I need a good makeup remover to get rid of smudges (*hello*, raccoon eyes). Conventional makeup removers come in small plastic bottles or individually-packaged, non-biodegradable wipes and seem to be either too drying or too greasy. It took a little experimenting, but I found a blend that is both gentle and effective. It's also nongreasy, won't sting your eyes, and easy to whip up when you're running low.

To make it, you just need safflower oil and witch hazel. You can find safflower oil in bulk or in a glass bottle, or use sweet almond oil, castor oil, jojoba oil, or sunflower oil in its place. I have only found witch hazel in a recyclable plastic bottle and I recommend buying the largest size available. Although it comes in plastic, you will only need a small amount to make the makeup remover and it will replace dozens of single-use bottles and countless disposable wipes.

**MAKES 4½ OUNCES**

### INGREDIENTS

3 tablespoons water

3 tablespoons safflower oil

3 tablespoons witch hazel

### SUPPLIES

Funnel (optional)

1 glass bottle (4½ ounce minimum) with cap

1. Using a funnel or a steady hand, pour the water, oil, and witch hazel into a small bottle. Cap the bottle and shake to combine the ingredients.

2. Apply a small amount to a reusable facial round and gently wipe your face to remove makeup.

# Apple Cider Conditioner

My favorite way to keep my hair soft and shiny is a homemade apple cider vinegar rinse. It naturally conditions hair, removes residue, and combats dandruff. The scent can be a little *salad-y* when your hair is wet, but I find that dissipates once my hair has dried. You could also add your favorite essential oil to help balance the vinegar's scent.

**MAKES 1¼ CUPS, ENOUGH FOR 1 OR 2 APPLICATIONS**

## INGREDIENTS

¼ cup apple cider vinegar

1 cup water

5 drops essential oil (optional)

## SUPPLIES

Funnel (optional)

glass bottle (16 ounce minimum) with cap or pour spout

1. Using a funnel, or a steady hand, pour the apple cider vinegar and water into a glass bottle. If you don't have a 16-ounce bottle, fill any container with a 1:4 ratio of apple cider vinegar to water.

2. Add essential oil to the bottle (if using). Cover the bottle and shake to combine.

3. After shampooing, pour a few tablespoons of conditioner onto your roots and gently massage your scalp. Leave it on your hair for 5 to 7 minutes.

4. Rinse, dry, and style your hair as usual.

# Hair Care

I used to be pretty high *mane*-tenance (see what I did there?). Around age sixteen, I dyed my hair jet black, then bleached it platinum blonde and had it chemically straightened (twice). I was addicted to my straightener and my bathroom was filled with expensive shampoos, conditioners, serums, and anything else that promised long, healthy hair. Ironically, my hair was so fried and damaged that by college, it stopped growing for three years.

If you had told my younger self that my hair routine in my thirties would entail using bar soap as shampoo, apple cider vinegar as conditioner, and air-drying in twisted pigtails (to enhance my natural curl), I wouldn't have believed you. My current routine is simpler and low waste, but my hair has never been longer or healthier. Not that everything is perfect—my hair is super long because I don't have time for haircuts (*thanks*, motherhood), my scalp can get flakey, and I always seem to have a rogue curl poking out.

My point here is, the easiest way to reduce waste with hair care is to work with what nature gave you and keep things simple.

**Shampoo.** Shampoo bars have become very popular in the zero-waste community. They usually come in a cardboard box or recyclable metal tin and they're great for travel. Much like regular bar soap, you lather the shampoo bar with your hands, massage the soap into your roots, and rinse. Shampoo bars tend to be less sudsy than commercial shampoos and your hair might need time to adjust. There is also a growing trend for *no poo*—washing your hair with baking soda or plain water and rinsing with apple cider vinegar. If shampoo bars and no poo aren't your jam, see whether your local bulk store offers shampoo refills, or buy the largest size bottle of your favorite brand (you can sometimes find shampoo in gallon-size jugs designed for salons).

**Conditioner.** If your hair seems dry and thirsty, try a homemade apple cider vinegar (ACV) rinse. This is one of the few beauty DIYs I swear by (it helps that it's only one ingredient). ACV makes your hair soft and shiny and removes built-up residue. It also helps balance your scalp's pH and combats dandruff. If vinegar doesn't appeal to you, try a conditioner bar, which is like a shampoo bar but applied to the ends of your hair. You can also buy liquid conditioner from Plaine Products or look for refill options in the bulk section.

**Serums and sprays.** If you want to smooth flyaways or moisturize ends, try a natural oil like argan, jojoba, coconut, or rosehip. You can also find serums in glass bottles. The great thing about using a natural oil is that it's multipurpose—use it to moisturize your face, body, and cuticles, and to remove makeup. For hair spray, make your own with vodka and lemon juice or, at the very least, recycle empty metal aerosol cans.

**Styling.** I don't do a lot of hair styling these days. I still have my curling iron and hair straightener tucked away in a drawer, but they're rarely used. Find what works for your hair. Maybe it's air-drying or styling your hair in a bun or braids, or maybe you keep using your hair styling tools. When your straightener or curling iron no longer works, look into recycling it at an e-waste drop-off (see my recycling guide on page 192). If you have a plastic hairbrush or comb in good working condition, keep using it. When you're ready for a replacement, switch to a compostable wood brush and comb. You'll love the way the wood bristles massage your scalp and they help reduce static.

**Hair ties.** For hair elastics, use what you have. There's also a growing trend in the zero-waste community to reuse hair elastics you find on the ground (after a good wash with soap, of course), but this ultra-thrifty option may not work for everyone. Traditional hair elastics are made from a mix of rubber, synthetic fabric, and a metal clasp. They belong in the trash once they break. If you want to buy a sustainable alternative, try KOOSHOO— their compostable hair ties are made from organic cotton and natural rubber.

# Personal Grooming

People sometimes associate environmentalism with living like a super-hippie, but choosing a zero-waste lifestyle doesn't mean you have to forgo personal grooming and ditch deodorant (though if that's your choice, no judgments here). From hair removal to body odor to nail care, there are low-waste alternatives that will keep you looking and feeling your best, while also breaking misconceptions about waste-free lifestyles.

**Deodorant.** For the most part, plastic deodorant sticks are non-recyclable. They're made from several different types of plastic that have to be separated and cleaned before they're placed in your curbside bin. You also have to make sure your waste department accepts each type of plastic, and even then, the pieces might be unrecognizable and sent to landfill. First, I recommend switching to a natural deodorant and skipping antiperspirant. Some people worry that switching to a "natural" deodorant equals a patchouli paste that doesn't actually work. My friends, natural deodorant has come a long way and there are even solutions that come in recyclable glass jars and compostable cardboard tubes—my favorites are Meow Meow Tweet and Fat and the Moon. Most natural deodorants use baking soda to kill odor-causing bacteria, but there are also options made with arrowroot powder for people with sensitive pits.

**Nails.** Part of zero-waste nail care is keeping things simple. I no longer get manicures or pedicures, but that doesn't mean I'll never paint my nails again, or that you have to go without. Keep your manicure eco-friendly by choosing nontoxic and vegan polish (I've also read about biodegradable options) and remove polish with a nontoxic remover sold in glass bottles with reusable cotton rounds.

---

**NAIL TOOLS**

**Cuticle cream.** Find a cream that comes in a metal tin or use a natural oil.

**Nailbrush.** Use a compostable wood brush with natural bristles to keep nails tidy.

**Nail file.** Keep nails neat and trim with a recyclable metal or glass file.

**Pumice stone.** Smooth rough soles with a natural pumice stone made from volcanic rock.

---

# Hair Removal

**Razors.** Safety razors have been around since the turn of the century and have recently resurged in popularity due to their low-waste profile. The razor is made from metal and uses a stainless-steel blade. Replacement blades are sold in a small cardboard box at the drugstore or online and can be recycled when you're done. It can take some practice to get used to using a safety razor, but with time, you'll love how it provides a close shave and prevents ingrown hairs. If a safety razor isn't for you, switch to a cartridge razor with a reusable handle and disposable blades (recycle used blades through TerraCycle).

**Wax.** Sugar waxing, or *sugaring,* is an easy and economical way to remove hair. This type of wax can be made at home with pantry ingredients; most recipes call for granulated sugar, lemon juice, and water. Once you've made the wax and it's cool enough to handle, apply the wax to your skin with your fingers then lift an edge to pull it off in one swift motion; you can also apply a cotton strip over the wax for better leverage. Both the wax and cotton strips are compostable when you're done.

---

## SAFETY RAZOR: DOS AND DON'TS

**Do** soften skin and hair follicles with hot water before shaving—a steamy shower or hot towel will do.

**Do** pull skin taut and shave at a 30- to 45-degree angle, with the grain (the direction hair grows).

**Do** collect used blades in a metal container, or a razor bank, before you recycle them—an exposed blade poses a safety risk to sanitary workers.

**Don't** forget to lather with shaving soap to reduce friction (bar and liquid soaps both work).

**Don't** apply pressure or pull the razor along the entire length of skin, as you see in commercials—it's a good way to cut yourself.

**Don't** travel with a safety razor in your carry-on bag; it may be confiscated. Check your bag or bring an old cartridge razor (or go without shaving during your trip).

# Health and Hygiene

I believe that protecting our individual health is our top priority, even over reducing waste. When we're not in good health, it becomes much harder to care for ourselves and others—let alone the environment. However, I also believe you can practice healthy living and good hygiene while minimizing plastic waste. Always use good judgment, do your research, find what works for you, and, when in doubt, consult a health care professional.

Never flush anything other than toilet paper down the toilet. Wipes marketed as *flushable* can actually clog toilets and sewer systems.

## TOILET PAPER

What are the most sustainable alternatives to toilet paper? Let's start with paper itself. Toilet paper is compostable, as is the cardboard tube in the center (you can also recycle the tube). Most packs come encased in a giant plastic bag, which can be recycled with soft plastic recycling. You could also switch to toilet paper that comes individually wrapped in paper, sold in a cardboard box. Who Gives a Crap delivers TP made from recycled schoolbooks to your doorstep. Additionally, adding a bidet attachment to your toilet will help reduce your toilet paper use.

Another popular item in zero-waste bathrooms is the "family cloth" or toilet "unpaper." Don't worry, a family cloth is not a single towel used by every member of your household. Rather, you add a basket of clean reusable cloths to your bathroom and use them in place of toilet paper for #1s. You could also use them for #2s, but they work best for this in conjunction with a bidet. When you're done, toss the used cloth into the hamper and wash with the laundry.

The next time you visit the dentist, politely refuse the goodie bag filled with toothpaste, floss, and other free samples. Let them know you are trying to reduce waste—you might inspire them to ditch the freebies.

## DENTAL

A dental routine that doesn't produce waste *and* keeps teeth and gums healthy? Yes, it does exist. From toothbrushes to toothpaste, floss to fresh breath, and even whiter teeth, there are sustainable dental hygiene alternatives that actually work. However, it's smart to review any changes to your oral care with a dentist first.

**Floss.** There are some serious issues with plastic floss. For one, it can become tangled up with marine life with devastating consequences. Additionally, many types of floss, especially ones marketed for their "glidability" are coated with perfluoroalkyl substances (PFAS), which have been linked to cancer and fertility issues. Swap plastic floss for silk floss. It's just like regular floss but it's compostable and comes in a refillable glass vial. You could also try an electronic water flosser. It squirts water between your teeth and around the gum line and is very effective at removing plaque and supporting healthy gums. They're also great for cleaning dental hardware, like braces. Although they're made from plastic, they replace dozens of plastic floss containers and hundreds of single-use dental picks. I use a portable water flosser made by Waterpik every night and silk floss every couple of days.

**Mouthwash.** To freshen breath, try making a homemade mouthwash. Most recipes include baking soda or hydrogen peroxide and essential oils. There are also mouthwash tablets that come in a recyclable glass jar. You dissolve one tablet into a glass of water and gargle as usual. Another option is oil pulling. Swishing oil around your mouth for 15 minutes helps remove bacteria, freshen breath, and whiten teeth. Many people use coconut oil for this, but you could also try olive, sunflower, or sesame oil.

**Toothbrush.** Consider this—every single plastic toothbrush you've ever used likely still exists (unless it was incinerated). If you calculate how many years you've been brushing your teeth, and multiply that number by how often you replace your brush (every two to three months on average), it adds up to . . . a lot. Fortunately, there are alternatives. Bamboo toothbrushes are made with a compostable handle and nylon bristles. When you're done, remove the bristles with pliers and send them to TerraCycle for recycling, or just snap off the head and compost the handle. You could also repurpose your toothbrush as part of a cleaning kit or convert the handles into garden markers. If you're attached to your electric toothbrush, fear not—I won't pry it out of your death grip. You can recycle electric toothbrush heads, as well as regular plastic toothbrushes, floss containers, and toothpaste tubes through Colgate's recycling program with TerraCycle—regardless of brand.

**Toothpaste.** Switching to a plastic-free toothpaste can be as easy as sprinkling baking soda onto your toothbrush. Baking soda is naturally abrasive and helps remove surface stains and freshen breath. If you don't like the taste or texture of straight baking soda (some people find it too salty), try toothpaste sold in a recyclable glass jar or metal tube—Georganics and Davids Natural Toothpaste are two of my favorite brands. Just clean the empty container or tube before you recycle it.

**Whitening.** To brighten your smile, try oil pulling (see mouthwash, page 79) or a homemade baking soda toothpaste. Since using baking soda to brush my teeth, I've noticed a whiter smile and less surface stains. You could also try a toothpaste that contains activated charcoal—the charcoal binds to plaque and removes stains, resulting in a whiter smile.

## EYE CARE

For those of you with some visual impairment (like me), sustainable options include glasses (most economical) or Lasik eye surgery (investment). If you're a contact lens wearer, you can recycle the blister packs and cardboard packaging. A blister pack consists of a hard plastic pod (usually #5 plastic) and a piece of aluminum foil. I separate the foil and save it to recycle in a larger ball of aluminum foil. Contact your curbside recycling program to see whether it accepts #5 plastic, or try to find a local drop-off (some Whole Foods Markets offer one). In terms of the contacts themselves, TerraCycle offers a free recycling program for used lenses and blister packs. You can also help extend the life of your contacts by alternating their use with eyeglasses or switching from dailies to a weekly or monthly version. For contact solution, there are no plastic-free options. Buy the largest-size bottle and recycle it when empty along with the cardboard packaging.

## MEDICAL

Your health is your number-one priority, waste or no waste. If you are sick and need medical attention or prescription medicine to get well, use it. That said, I think (and I *believe* a doctor would agree) that taking good care of your body through a healthy lifestyle—well-balanced diet, proper hydration, daily exercise, and rest—can help reduce your need for medical attention and supplies. Here are a few more ideas to reduce medical waste.

Never flush expired medication down the toilet—it can contaminate your water system. Many hospitals offer a drop-off, or your local waste service may offer a pick-up program.

**Pills and vitamins.** Choose medications and vitamins that come in recyclable glass bottles over plastic, when possible. The safety seal is trash, but you can compost the cotton ball that comes inside the bottle and recycle the cardboard box. Also, don't buy too big of a bottle—it may expire before you can use it. Avoid individual blister packs, if you can, which are made from mixed materials and can't be recycled. Prescription medicine bottles are typically made from #5 plastic and may be accepted by your curbside recycling or you can look for a drop-off.

---

# FIRST AID

**Bandages.** Use up your current supply of plastic bandages; when you're out, switch to a compostable version made from organic bamboo fiber by PATCH. You could also use compostable cotton gauze.

**Burns.** Cut open an aloe leaf and apply the gel inside to soothe a burn. If you don't have access to an aloe plant, try to find aloe gel in a recyclable glass bottle or jar.

**Cramps and aches.** For body aches and cramps, fill a reusable rubber bottle with hot water or use an electric heating pad for relief.

**Swelling.** Make your own ice pack by placing ice from a stainless-steel or silicone ice tray in a reusable silicone bag. You could also use a stainless-steel ice pack made by Onyx Containers.

# 5 Zero-Waste Ways to Fight a Cold

Cold season. You know it's coming—you've washed your hands religiously, avoided your sneezing coworker like the plague, and treated your body like a temple—but you still come down with a nasty bug. Although most cold medicines are packaged in unrecyclable blister packs and many curbside programs don't accept prescription bottles, always follow medical advice for something serious. For the common cold, old-fashioned tried-and-true remedies are often most effective, affordable, and a low-waste way to get better soon.

1. **Sip something soothing.** Sipping hot teas and broths is not only comforting during a cold, it also helps break up mucus and clear congestion. It also helps prevent dehydration and soothes a sore throat. Lemon is a good source of vitamin C and helps reduce inflammation. Ginger is an anti-inflammatory with antibiotic properties that boost the immune system. Local raw honey relieves congestion and is a natural cough suppressant. Here's an easy, soothing remedy: Slice 1 inch of ginger into rounds and soak in 2 cups of hot water. Add the juice of half a lemon and stir in 1 teaspoon of honey. Strain and drink.

2. **Soak in salts.** A steamy bath is a traditional remedy for reducing a fever. Epsom salt in your bath can help ease muscle aches, reduce inflammation, and detoxify your body. Because skin is highly porous, adding Epsom salt, full of minerals like magnesium and sulfate, to your bathwater can literally draw harmful toxins out of your body. Buy salts in bulk and add a few drops of lavender or eucalyptus essential oil to aid relaxation.

3. **Oil of oregano.** Oil of oregano has strong antibacterial and antiviral properties and has been used since ancient Greek and Roman times as a natural remedy for respiratory issues, including coughs, colds, the flu, sore throats, and bronchitis. You can buy oil of oregano at many natural foods stores in a glass vial—not to be confused with oregano essential oil, which is more concentrated and shouldn't be ingested. Place 3 drops of oil of oregano under your tongue twice daily until the symptoms are gone—but beware, it's pungent stuff. Keep a glass of water nearby in case the taste is too strong.

4. **Sleep with a scarf.** Wearing a scarf when you're sick is a traditional German remedy. The theory is that the scarf slightly raises the temperature of your throat, drawing immune cells to the area and helping speed the recovery process. I've found using a scarf at bedtime helps relieve a sore throat by morning.

5. **Flush mucus.** I hate nothing more than trying to sleep when I'm sick and congestion makes it difficult to breathe. My solution—the neti pot. Flushing your nasal passages with warm saltwater may sound unappealing, but it really helps break up mucus so you can finally *breathe*. It also rinses away dust, pollen, and other irritants and supports a healthy upper respiratory system. I like it because it reduces sinus pressure and headaches when you're congested. You can pick up a ceramic neti pot at most health food stores. The US Food and Drug Administration recommends using distilled, sterile, or boiled (then cooled) water to protect yourself from bacteria and protozoa.

Ditch paper tissues and switch to a cloth handkerchief for a runny nose. Handkerchiefs are not only reusable, they feel much nicer on sensitive skin. You could also use a cloth napkin or an unpaper towel.

# Menstruation and Family Planning

Even when it comes to the most intimate areas of our bodies, there are simple ways to reduce plastic and protect your reproductive health. These low-waste alternatives for personal care can make feeling good feel even better.

### PERIODS

What do you look for in menstrual hygiene products . . . something discreet, comfortable, affordable? What about good for your body, or at least not harmful? Unfortunately, most menstrual hygiene options contain chemicals and toxins you wouldn't want getting cozy with your private parts. Many commercial pads and tampons contain rayon, dioxins, fragrance, volatile organic compounds, pesticides, and BPAs, which have been linked to cancer, birth defects, infertility, and hormone disruption.

Conventional menstrual hygiene products also harm our planet. According to an article in *National Geographic*, the average person will use more than 15,000 tampons or pads throughout their lifetime, most of which end up in landfill. But, what if I told you there's another way to prevent leaks that produces zero waste, won't harm your body, and even makes for a better user experience? And just think, no more emergency tampon runs to the drugstore!

**Menstrual cup.** The menstrual cup is a bell-shaped silicone cup that fits inside the vagina to collect your flow. You remove the cup when it's full (up to 12 hours), empty the contents into the sink, toilet, or shower, and give it a quick rinse before reinserting. Some people are squeamish about switching to a cup and it can take some practice to get used to inserting and removing it. But I can't tell you how many times I've heard that a user's only regret is not switching to a menstrual cup sooner. A menstrual cup collects more blood than a tampon, so it's very effective at preventing leaks while also being comfortable to wear. It can also feel incredibly empowering to care for your period in a way that's healthy and sustainable.

**Organic pads and tampons.** If you're not ready to part with traditional tampons and pads, look for brands made from 100 percent organic cotton with a compostable cardboard applicator, or no applicator. Products made from nonorganic cotton are typically treated with pesticides, not something you want near a highly absorbent area of your body.

Reusable menstrual products can seem expensive compared to disposable versions. But, when you compare the lifetime cost, you'll see the investment pays for itself within the first year. A menstrual cup costs between $30 and $40 and can last up to ten years compared to $60 to $120 for a one-year supply of tampons or pads (roughly $1,800 over a lifetime).

**Reusable pads and undies.** Did you know that one average sanitary pad contains the equivalent of four plastic bags? Reusable pads are washable and come in a variety of shapes and thicknesses—from a daily panty liner to a super-absorbent overnight pad. Instead of sticking to your underwear, they fasten around the gusset with snaps or hook-and-loop closure wings. You might also try period panties. The underwear comes in a range of styles from boy shorts to thongs and directly absorbs menstrual blood. Some designs can hold up to two tampons' worth of liquid, or you could use the underwear as backup to a menstrual cup. When you're done, toss the pad or underwear in the wash with your normal load, but be sure to note what the fabric is made from. Synthetic materials shed plastic microfibers, which can be caught and disposed of with a specially designed washing bag like Guppyfriend.

## FAMILY PLANNING

Let's talk about sex. Practicing safe sex and protecting your body from STIs are *way* more important than minimizing waste. And, preventing an unwanted pregnancy is *way* more eco-friendly than producing another human (even if you use a mountain of condoms in the process). That said, there are a few simple ways to make your sex life more earth friendly, and dare I say, more pleasurable.

**Condoms.** Condoms are designed to be one and done; they should never be reused. The only biodegradable condoms are made from lambskin (a sheep's intestine), though you do have to factor the environmental cost of raising a sheep, and they don't protect you from STIs. Latex is made from natural rubber that comes from a tree, so a 100 percent latex condom will eventually break down. Unfortunately, most latex condoms are made from a mix of latex and other materials that aren't biodegradable. You can recycle the cardboard packaging in your regular curbside pick-up, and the wrapper through TerraCycle, but used condoms should always be thrown away. Also, never flush them down the toilet—they can clog sewage systems.

**IUDs.** One of the most eco-friendly and effective forms of birth control is an intrauterine device (IUD)—a thin, flexible T-shaped device inserted into the uterus that lasts anywhere from three to twelve years, depending on the brand. There are two types of IUDs—hormonal and copper. The hormonal IUD is made from flexible plastic and releases a very low dose of progestin. The copper IUD is also made from plastic with a coil of copper wrapped around the stem. The copper version contains no hormones, but it might cause heavier bleeding and cramping.

Instead of using paper tissues or disposable wet wipes to clean up after intimacy, try a cloth towel. It's softer on your skin and reusable, and *everything* will wash out in the laundry.

**Rhythm method.** Using the rhythm method, or fertility awareness, you keep track of the days you are ovulating with a calendar by measuring your basal body temperature or mucus discharge. During fertile days, you either abstain from sex or use birth control, then have unprotected sex (provided you and your partner have both been tested for STIs) on nonfertile days. This method works best for people with a predictable cycle, who are diligent about tracking their fertility. This method does not protect you from STIs. I started using the rhythm method by tracking my basal body temperature through the Natural Cycles app on my smartphone. I take my temperature each morning while still in bed, and have found it to be very effective for both preventing pregnancy and getting pregnant when my husband and I were ready.

**Lube.** Conventional lubricants can contain petroleum, which is made from crude oil (*not sexy*). Additionally, lube comes packaged in wasteful plastic tubes or packets. Switch to something more natural, like coconut oil, olive oil, sweet almond oil, or aloe vera. You can also buy natural lubricants sold in glass bottles, including formulas with CBD, which have been said to enhance pleasure. Always determine what your condom is made from before you lube up; some oils can damage latex and should be used with nonlatex birth control methods.

**Toys.** If you're looking for a sex toy, the most important thing to consider is the material it's made from. Stick to body- and planet-safe options such as silicone, wood, and glass and opt for rechargeable toys and batteries. If your toy has expired, or you're ready to ditch the plastic ones, mail it in for recycling through EdenFantasys (based in the United States) or Lovehoney (based in the United Kingdom). Additionally, there is a new vibrator available from Gaia Eco made from starch-based bioplastic.

Cyclical studies have shown that the Natural Cycles rhythm method is 93 percent effective at preventing unwanted pregnancy with typical use, putting it on par with hormonal birth control pills (91 percent). It is also more effective than condoms (82 percent), but less effective than IUDs (almost 100 percent).

## You Can Compost That

Many homes limit recycling and compost to the kitchen, but there are multiple compostable items found in the bathroom, too. Just add a dedicated bin or jar, or best yet, repurpose your trash bucket.

- Bamboo toothbrush, with nylon bristles removed
- Beard trimmings
- Cardboard tampon applicators and paper wrappers
- Cotton balls
- Cotton swabs (cardboard or bamboo sticks only)
- Hair
- Lambskin condoms
- Menstrual pads and tampons (100 percent cotton only)
- Nail clippings
- Natural loofahs
- Silk dental floss
- Tissue
- Toilet paper
- Toilet paper tubes

# Plastic-Free(ish) Action Plan

| 🏆 | 🏆 |
|---|---|
| **SMALL WINS** | **BIG WINS** |
| • Simplify your hair care routine and use up products that you already have.<br><br>• Ditch disposable razors for a cartridge razor with a reusable handle.<br><br>• Use organic cotton tampons with a cardboard applicator and paper wrapper and compost everything when you're done.<br><br>• Buy recycled toilet paper in a cardboard box with no plastic packaging.<br><br>• Add a compost bin to your bathroom for used tissue, cotton swabs, cotton balls, and hair. | • Switch to a shampoo bar, buy shampoo in bulk, or try no poo.<br><br>• Try a safety razor with recyclable blades, sugar waxing, or go *au naturel*.<br><br>• Switch to a menstrual cup or try reusable pads or period panties and toss them in the wash when you're done.<br><br>• Add a bidet attachment to your toilet or switch to cloth toilet unpaper.<br><br>• Get rid of your trash bucket altogether and compost or recycle everything. |

# CLEANING

I used to be a cleaning products collector. I believed every room, surface, and fabric needed its own special cleanser and that having an arsenal of supplies was the *adult* thing to do. There were the usual suspects—all-purpose spray, glass cleaner, tub scrub, mopping solution—along with specialized cleansers for laptop screens, granite, stainless steel, and wood. To complete my set, I had an assortment of tools: two kinds of mops, plastic sponges, magic erasers, a pet vacuum, disinfecting wipes, and loads of paper towels. You get the picture.

I tried to favor "green" supplies whenever possible but, deep down, I suspected that conventional cleaners (aka chemicals) were necessary to get things *truly* clean and sanitary. I figured they must be safe enough and ignored the warning labels—"harmful if swallowed," "skin and eye irritant," "keep out of reach of children." Some products emitted fumes and fragrances so potent I had to leave the house while it aired out, but the residue was there as I prepped food or bathed in the tub. And, when I found the scent too strong or the cleaner seemed ineffective, I tossed it in the trash or poured it down the drain, not putting much thought into where it would end up.

If you're ready to part with a few of your chemical cleaners, think twice before dumping them in the trash or down the drain, where they can contaminate water sources and the environment. Many communities offer a hazardous waste drop-off or pick-up during designated times of year—check your local waste management website to find out which cleaning supplies they accept.

How did we get *here*? Our grandparents were thrifty and resourceful and kept homes spick-and-span with little more than vinegar, baking soda, and elbow grease. When did we ditch these tried-and-true supplies for an army of designer chemicals? Since going zero waste, I've rediscovered the magic cleaning power of these natural solutions—if they're good enough for the bubbies, they're good enough for me. I've also become more suspicious of conventional cleaners since becoming a parent—my son puts *everything* in his mouth and I'd rather have him lick dirt than chemical residue.

Fortunately, there are plenty of natural, affordable, and effective ways to clean your home—top to bottom—without harsh chemicals or disposable supplies. I will share a few simple DIY cleaners using no more than two ingredients (that you likely already have in your pantry), and note brands offering plastic-free solutions, when applicable. You'll achieve a sparkling clean home without harming your health or the planet and discover supplies so sustainable *and* beautiful you might start looking for excuses to tidy (No promises, okay?).

# Zero-Waste Cleaning Kit

Simplifying your cleaning kit is not only better for your health and the environment, it also saves money and frees valuable storage space (*goodbye*, ugly plastic bottles). These natural cleaning alternatives can be used to keep your home spotless without plastic waste or harmful chemicals. The cleaners also work just as well, if not better, than their toxic counterparts.

## THE ESSENTIALS

1. **Baking soda.** Baking soda is a natural abrasive and deodorizer and an essential ingredient for cleaning DIYs. Buy it in bulk in a glass jar or recyclable cardboard box.

2. **Castile soap.** This gentle plant-derived soap is biodegradable and often can be found for purchase in bulk. You could also use a Castile bar soap and convert it into liquid cleanser when needed.

3. **Cloth rags.** You're going to need rags (*lots* of rags) or unpaper towels. Keep it zero waste by making your own from worn T-shirts, bedsheets, and bath towels.

4. **Glass bottles.** Fill with homemade cleaning supplies, bulk soaps, and even plain water for ironing. You could also fit a repurposed beverage bottle with a spray nozzle, soap pump, or pour spout of choice.

5. **Toothbrush.** A toothbrush's thick bristles and small head are perfect for cleaning grout and other tight areas, and it's a nice way to reuse an old brush that's past its prime.

6. **White vinegar.** Vinegar is the backbone of a clean home and can be used to remove stains, kill bacteria, and deodorize. Buy it in the largest jug available or a glass bottle.

7. **Wood scrub brush.** Ditch your nasty plastic sponge for a natural wood scrub brush. It lasts longer, looks nicer, and can be composted at the end of its useful life.

## THE EXTRAS

8. **Essential oils.** Add a few drops to All-Purpose Cleaner (page 97), wool laundry balls, or even a spray bottle of water for a fresh scent. My favorites are lavender, eucalyptus, and sandalwood.

9. **Funnel.** This is a handy tool for decanting soaps and homemade cleaning supplies into bottles, or skip it and use a steady hand.

Microfiber cloths are popular for lint-free cleaning, but they shed plastic fibers that end up in the ocean. Select rags made from natural fibers like cotton, hemp, and bamboo and compost the lint after drying or reuse as a fire starter.

# HOW DO I CLEAN THAT?

**Appliances.** Wet a rag with hot water, then wipe down appliances to clear away grease and bits of food. Next, liberally spray with All-Purpose Cleaner (opposite page) and wipe clean with a dry rag. Use baking soda and a toothbrush to scrub any stubborn areas.

**Baking sheets.** Restore grimy baking sheets to their original luster with a simple DIY. Plug your sink and add ½ cup of baking soda, ½ cup of white vinegar, and enough hot water to submerge the pans. Let soak for up to an hour, then scrub clean.

**Cast iron.** First things first—*never* wash cast iron with soap because it can destroy the seasoning that makes the cast iron a naturally nonstick surface. Instead, use a stiff-bristle brush or copper scrubber with hot water. Use a cloth rag with a tiny amount of cooking oil to dry and season the pan until it's dark and glistening.

**Counters.** An All-Purpose Cleaner (opposite page) works for most countertops, with the exception of soft stones like marble, which can become etched from the acidic vinegar. Instead, use a cloth rag with hot water and a little bit of dish soap.

**Fridge.** A near-empty fridge is easier to clean, so start by purging and composting expired foods (and recycling packaging whenever possible). Then, spray the interior with All-Purpose Cleaner (opposite page) and wipe clean with a dry rag. I like to line my crisper drawers with folded tea towels to collect leftover pieces of produce and for easy cleanup.

**Wood tools.** Hand wash wood utensils and cutting boards with warm soapy water and dry with a cloth towel. Never let wood soak or run it through the dishwasher—water causes wood to warp and splinter. Use raw linseed oil, walnut oil, or beeswax to moisturize and protect the wood.

# All-Purpose Cleaner

I never thought that All-Purpose Cleaner, made with a single ingredient, would replace the majority of my household cleaning supplies. I use it for *everything*—counters, fridge, toilets, showers, windows, mirrors, floors, pet accidents—you name it. You may be thinking, "If I use vinegar to clean my house, won't it smell like a pickle jar?" Personally, I don't mind the scent and have found that it dissipates once dry. For a less vinegary aroma, add a few drops of your favorite essential oil to the bottle.

**MAKES 16 OUNCES**

## INGREDIENTS

½ cup white vinegar

10 drops essential oil (lavender or eucalyptus), lemon and orange rinds, or rosemary sprigs (optional)

## SUPPLIES

Funnel (optional)

1 glass spray bottle (16 ounce)

1. Using a funnel, or a steady hand, pour the vinegar into your spray bottle.

2. Add 10 drops of your favorite essential oil, or infuse your spray by adding lemon or orange rinds or rosemary sprigs to the bottle.

3. Fill the rest of the bottle with water. Add the spray head to the bottle and give it a shake. To clean, just spray and wipe!

# Check Out My Zero-Waste Kitchen Sink

1. Clean dishes with a **wood dish brush** instead of a plastic sponge.

2. Use a **copper scrubber** to loosen stubborn bits of food from cast-iron skillets and pans.

3. Wash dishes and hands with **Castile soap** bought in bulk in a glass bottle.

4. Use a **cloth rag** to wipe counters after food prep and crumbs after meals.

5. Use a recyclable **metal or wood dish rack** or hand dry dishes with a cotton tea towel.

6. A **minimal countertop** makes it easier to cook and tidy.

# Kitchen Cleaning

There's no question that a clean kitchen is more inviting to cook in. From dishwashing to appliances and countertops, here are some recommendations to keep your kitchen tidy and low waste.

## DISHWASHING TOOLS

You know what's the absolute worst?—when you've finished washing dishes and realize your hands smell like an old sponge. One of my favorite zero-waste swaps was replacing my slimy dish sponge with a compostable wood brush. Wood brushes feature natural bristles that won't trap food or bacteria and keep hands smelling great. They're also long lasting, nice to look at, and can be composted when you're ready for a replacement.

**Bottle brush.** The rounded head is perfect for cleaning glasses, water bottles, and scrubbing the grooves of pots and dishes. My personal favorite at home.

**Copper scrubber.** For tough jobs, especially cast iron, try a copper scouring pad—they easily remove stubborn bits of food and are recyclable at the end of their useful life.

**Dish brush.** Features a long wood handle to keep hands dry and a removable head that can be composted and swapped for a replacement, as needed.

**Pot brush.** This petite, but mighty, brush features a curved wood handle that fits into the palm of your hand and stiff Tampico bristles made from plant fibers.

**Tawashi brush.** This traditional Japanese brush is made from durable palm fibers wrapped around a metal wire. It's great for cleaning dishes, pots, and vegetables.

For any service that offers "zero-waste" or "eco-friendly" cleaning supplies mailed to your home, ask questions and do your research before signing up. Sometimes the "recyclable" packaging (such as cardboard cartons) includes a plastic lining or other materials that aren't accepted in many curbside pick-ups.

## DISH SOAP

Have you ever wondered why most kitchens have dish soap *and* hand soap? Isn't soap, well, *soap*? It turns out many conventional dish soaps are filled with harsh chemicals that not only strip natural oils and dry out hands, they can also harm our health. Some common ingredients to avoid are chlorine, ammonia, formaldehyde, and things noted with vague terms like fragrance and colorant. These chemicals can also slip through water treatment plants, polluting water sources and threatening marine life. Here are some sustainable alternatives to consider that are also gentler on hands and the environment.

**Bulk liquid soap.** If you prefer liquid soap, buy it in bulk in a glass jar. If bulk options aren't available, buy a gallon jug or the largest size you can find and decant it into a smaller glass bottle. Also, you don't have to buy a special dish soap—try liquid Castile, like Dr. Bronner's. My one tip is that Castile tends to be runnier than conventional dish soap and doesn't always work well with a standard soap pump—you may want to try a glass bottle with a pour spout instead. Fillaree also offers dish soap in a glass bottle with a refill option and subscription service.

**Dish soap bar.** Consider swapping liquid dish soap for bar soap. Olive oil-based soaps like Aleppo and Savon de Marseille have been used for centuries to clean everything from dishes to hands, hair, and even laundry. You could also use a Castile bar soap or a bar specially made for dishwashing from No Tox Life. Bar soap creates suds just like liquid soap and comes packaged in a cardboard box, wrapped in paper, or package free. You simply rub your cleaning brush on the bar to form a lather and wash your dishes as usual. You'll be surprised by how beautiful a simple bar of soap looks next to your sink.

**Dishwasher detergent.** If you're lucky, you may be able to find dishwashing powder in bulk. If that isn't an option, opt for powdered soap or tablets in a recyclable cardboard box with no plastic liner or scoop, like Seventh Generation, If You Care, and Ecover. There are also a growing number of businesses offering plastic-free tablets mailed in recyclable or compostable packaging, including Clean Cult and Dropps. If you want to give your dishes extra shine, white vinegar can be used as a rinse aid to remove hard-water stains. Pour one cup of vinegar into a bowl and place it on the top rack of your dishwasher (adding it directly to the rinse aid compartment can corrode the plastic parts). The vinegar will also clean and disinfect the dishwasher itself.

# Bathroom Cleaning

Natural materials and uncluttered surfaces can make your bathroom feel like a luxurious spa.

**Cleaning rags.** I like to keep a stack of clean cloth rags in our bathroom vanity to wipe the sink, medicine cabinet, and mirror, and mop up after toothbrushing and washing my face. I'm more likely to keep the bathroom tidy when cleaning supplies are nearby. I also keep an extra bottle of All-Purpose Cleaner (page 97) in the vanity.

**Hand soap.** No need to buy a special soap to wash hands. Just add a simple bar of soap to a well-drained dish by the sink or place the bar on a natural loofah pad, which collects soap residue and doubles as a bathroom scrubber. You could also fill a glass bottle with liquid Castile soap, which works for washing hands, hair, and body, and for general cleaning up.

**Scrub brush.** A natural wood scrub brush can be helpful for cleaning floors, tubs, showers, sinks, and more. I use one that has an S-shape, for a better grip, and stiff bristles for cleaning stubborn mildew and soap scum. I also like to occasionally use a bamboo toothbrush to clean grout and tight edges of the sink and vanity.

**Toilet brush.** There's no way around it—toilet brushes get grungy and have to be tossed every once in a while. When your sad plastic brush is ready for a replacement, swap it with a wood toilet brush. Wood brushes are long lasting and compostable when it's time to say goodbye (they also look much nicer than plastic). You can store your brush in a specially made wood stand to air-dry between uses, or stick it in a metal pitcher for extra discretion.

# HOW DO I CLEAN THAT?

**Grout.** Tiles are a great way to add personality and texture to a small space. The only tricky part is keeping the grout clean. Whisk ¼ cup of baking soda with a few teaspoons of dish soap until it forms a paste. Apply the paste to the grout and spray with All-Purpose Cleaner (page 97). Let it sit for 10 minutes, then scrub with an old toothbrush and wipe clean with a damp rag.

**Soap scum.** Soap scum forms when soap interacts with hard water. To remove it, combine one part vinegar and one part dish soap in a spray bottle. Liberally spray the solution onto the surface you want to clean. Let it sit for 10 minutes, then rinse with water and wipe clean with a dry rag.

**Toilet.** Spray All-Purpose Cleaner (page 97) into the bowl, let it sit for 10 minutes, then scrub with a toilet brush. For tougher stains, sprinkle baking soda into the bowl before you spray in the cleaner, then scrub. You can also use all-purpose spray and a cloth rag to clean the exterior of the toilet.

## AIR FRESHENERS

**Baking soda.** In a glass Mason jar, combine ½ cup of baking soda and a few drops of essential oil, like lemon or rosemary. Swap the metal lid for breathable cloth fabric held in place by the metal ring or reuse a rubber band.

**Candle.** Light a sustainably sourced beeswax or soy wax candle to clear unwanted odors. No need for added fragrance IMO.

**Essential oils.** Add your favorite essential oil, like rose, lavender or eucalyptus, to a spray bottle full of water and spritz bad smells (and vibes) away.

**Indoor plants.** Plants can help neutralize odors and remove toxins. Add a spider plant, snake plant, or aloe vera plant in a simple terra-cotta or ceramic pot.

# DIY Tub and Sink Scrub

Our tub gets daily use since my husband and I had a baby. After a week of bathing, I start to notice a scummy ring around the bottom. Although a commercial tub scrub would probably do the trick, I don't love the thought of bathing my son in chemical residue. After a little research, I discovered that just baking soda and a squeeze of dish soap make an excellent tub scrub. You don't even have to measure it—just eyeball it. It takes just under one minute to prepare and will leave your tub sparkling clean with minimal effort. It also works for cleaning sinks.

**MAKES 1 APPLICATION**

**INGREDIENTS**

2 tablespoons baking soda

1 tablespoon liquid soap (Castile or dish soap)

**SUPPLIES**

Cloth rag (for acrylic tubs)

Scrub brush (for cast-iron tubs)

## ACRYLIC TUB

1. Add baking soda to a small dish.

2. Whisk in liquid soap with a fork until a thick paste forms.

3. Dip a dry cloth into the paste and wipe your tub until it's clean.

4. Rinse with water.

## CAST-IRON TUB OR SINK

1. Rinse the area you plan to clean.

2. Sprinkle baking soda over the area. Let sit for 10 minutes.

3. Drizzle liquid soap over the area.

4. Scrub with a stiff-bristle brush.

5. Rinse with water.

# Floors and Windows

You don't need harsh chemicals to keep floors sparkling clean. Just add ½ cup of white vinegar to a bucket of hot water with a few drops of your favorite essential oil for optional aromatherapy.

## FLOORS

When your plastic-y tools have kicked the bucket (ha), try these sustainable swaps.

**Broom.** Opt for a wood-handled broom with natural bristles made from corn husks, silk, horsehair, or yucca. Pair it with a metal dustpan.

**Mop.** Replace disposable Swiffer pads with a reusable cover or try a Cuban mop–a T-shaped wood stick you can use with any cotton towel or rag.

**Vacuum.** Choose a bagless version and remember to compost the contents after removing anything that's inorganic.

## WINDOWS

Remove smudgy fingerprints with All-Purpose Cleaner (page 97) and crumpled up newspaper (for a lint-free shine). Truthfully, we don't often have newspaper lying around, so I typically use a cloth rag.

# Laundry

I have to admit something—I love doing laundry (Don't tell my family, okay?). Digging my hands into a warm pile of clothes, inhaling the scent of freshly laundered shirts, perfecting my KonMari fold while binging my favorite reality shows. Sign me up. The good news—removing plastic from most of your laundry routine is simple.

# Zero-Waste Laundry Kit

If there's one thing I don't like about laundry, it's trying to find a zero-waste laundry detergent I actually like. I've tried everything from a concentrated bar that dissolves in water to an eco-friendly detergent that came in a compostable jug, with varied results. All of this is to say that finding the right plastic-free detergent for your home might take some trial and error, and results may depend on your washer and water type, the nature of the stain, fabrics, and a variety of other factors. My advice is to start by looking for biodegradable detergents and test a small amount before you invest in a larger supply. Once you find a detergent you like, assembling the rest of your zero-waste laundry kit is a piece of cake

## THE ESSENTIALS

1. **Fabric softener.** A cup of vinegar can be added to the rinse cycle to soften clothes naturally. And don't worry, your clothes won't smell like salad. It can also be used to deodorize mildew-y towels, cloth diapers, and rags used to clean up pet accidents.

2. **Natural laundry detergent.** You can find commercial brands of powdered detergent sold in a recyclable box (though they often come with a plastic scoop) or try Meliora's natural detergent sold in a refillable and recyclable metal can. Biodegradable detergent pods made by Dropps are available online. If you're feeling adventurous, make your own or try soap nuts.

3. **Stain remover.** Instead of a stain-removing spray, try a bar of soap. Simply spritz the area with water and rub the bar into the stain. You could also try Meliora's stain stick, which comes packaged in a cardboard box.

4. **Washing bag.** Did you know that clothes continuously shed small plastic fibers that end up in the ocean? Wash synthetic fabrics such as polyester, nylon, rayon, and spandex in Guppyfriend—a mesh bag that traps plastic microfibers so they don't contaminate our natural environment.

## THE EXTRAS

5. **Lint brush.** Sticky lint rollers are wasteful—both the sheets and wand are trash. Switch to a reusable lint brush with a wood handle and natural rubber bristles. The rubber attracts hair and dust and can be rinsed between uses.

6. **Wool dryer balls.** Reduce drying time and energy use with wool dryer balls. The balls prevent static and help soften clothes naturally. Add essential oils to the balls to give your clothes a fresh scent. They last for an estimated one thousand loads and can be composted at the end of life.

CONTINUED

7. **Bleach alternatives.** (Not pictured.) Swap harsh chlorine bleach for natural whiteners like boiling water and lemon juice, baking soda, or my favorite—solar energy! After washing, place the item in direct sunlight to dry and watch stains disappear.

8. **Sweater stone.** How do you fix a fuzzy sweater without removing each pill by hand? Try a sweater stone—a natural stone, usually made from pumice, that you gently brush along the fabric to remove pills and fuzz.

## AIR-DRYING

To save energy and money, skip the dryer. Give damp clothes a good shake to smooth out wrinkles and hang on a clothesline or portable rack to dry (or if you're like me, on the backs of chairs, hooks, and anything else you can find). Another benefit of air-drying is it's better for your clothes. All that tumbling and exposure to high heat can snag and damage materials (not to mention shrink your favorite sweater). Air-drying is the best way to preserve fabrics and extend the life of your garments. Also, sunshine is a natural disinfectant and brightener and is more gentle and effective than bleach at removing stains from towels, sheets, and cloth diapers. But, be careful about leaving dark clothes in the sun too long; it can fade colors.

## DRY CLEANING

Most dry cleaners use a solvent called perchloroethylene, or perc—considered a health and environmental hazard by the US Environmental Protection Agency. Look for a dry cleaner who uses wet cleaning or liquid carbon dioxide to remove stains. Be sure to ask for the specific methods and chemicals they use—stores that advertise "green," "organic," and "eco-friendly" methods could just be *greenwashing*. Additionally, ask whether your cleaner offers a reusable garment bag so you can skip the plastic bag or provide your own. If plastic is unavoidable, recycle the bag at a soft plastic drop-off. Also, remember to return metal hangers when you pick up clothes so they can be reused by your dry cleaner.

Aim for a full washing machine each time you run a load of laundry to save water and energy. Also, use cold water whenever possible—it saves energy and helps preserve fabrics and colors.

# You Can Compost That

- Broom sweepings
- Cloth rags
  (cut into small strips)
- Crumbs
- Dead bugs
- Dryer lint
  (natural fabrics only)
- Dust bunnies
- Feathers
- Fireplace ash
- Flowers
- Houseplant trimmings
- Paper masking tape
- Paper towels and cardboard roll
- Pet fur
- Vacuum contents
  (inorganic material
  removed first)
- Wood cleaning brushes
  (with natural bristles)

# 5 Zero-Waste Ways to Declutter for a Cleaner Home

Installing new shelves, increasing storage, and buying fancy supplies aren't the keys to cultivating a minimal home. Rather, it's about mindfully reducing belongings and preventing new ones from taking their place. One of the biggest similarities between minimalism and zero waste is they both train us to become mindful consumers. When we reduce the items we have, we are more likely to treat our remaining belongings with care. We also become more cautious about new purchases and may favor better quality products that last longer than disposables. Another benefit of having a minimal, organized home is that it helps ease anxiety and allows us to think more clearly; it also makes it easier to tidy. Which is easier to clean—a bare kitchen counter or a counter covered with appliances, knickknacks, junk mail, and other miscellaneous objects? Here are a few tips for reducing clutter the zero-waste way.

1. **Don't buy organizing supplies.** We've all seen those beautifully organized craft closets and playrooms with color-coded plastic bins. Although it can be tempting to buy a bunch of supplies to stay organized, it should be the very last step after decluttering—and I recommend putting it off as long as possible. Containers and baskets can be helpful for corralling certain objects, but you may find something you can repurpose instead, like a metal tea tin or cardboard gift boxes. If you do need supplies, look for them secondhand and favor sustainable materials, like wood trays and woven baskets.

2. **Purge thoughtfully.** Dispose of your belongings as thoughtfully as possible. Your local thrift shop probably doesn't want your chipped mugs or dirty sneakers. Although some things have to be tossed, some items can be recycled (see my recycling guide on page 192). You can also list items for free on Craigslist, Facebook Marketplace, and buy-sell-trade (BST) groups. If you feel guilty about parting with something valuable, try selling it through your local consignment shop or resale sites such as Poshmark and eBay.

3. **Remove everything.** Whether you're organizing an entire closet or just your sock drawer, you need to be able to see the full assortment before you start purging. Grouping all your clothes, accessories, and undergarments into one pile gives you a more accurate assessment of how much you own and helps you be more selective about what to keep. It also provides an opportunity to clean your closet or drawers thoroughly before refilling them—give everything a good wipe and repair anything that's damaged while you're at it.

4. **Do it often.** Although decluttering might seem daunting at first, the more you do it, the easier it becomes. Even though our home is pretty minimal and we do ongoing purges, I'm always coming across things we can do without (though I'm happy to report the pile has been shrinking). Keep dedicated donate, sell, and recycle bins to add to as you identify items you're ready to part with.

5. **Make it manageable.** Decluttering takes time and patience (and good music and snacks). Instead of devoting an entire day to a giant project, consider dividing it into manageable chunks— "Today, I will tackle my junk drawer and tomorrow, the pantry!" I love this tip from Shira Gill, one of my favorite minimalists and home organizers: She recommends a "15-minute win"—setting a timer for 15 minutes to tackle a project. Shortening the amount of time you devote to decluttering helps keep you fresh and motivated.

# DECLUTTERING: DOS AND DON'TS

✓ **Do** tackle one small project at a time—break up huge tasks like organizing your garage or kitchen into more manageable chunks.

✓ **Do** donate items in good working condition to thrift and consignment shops or sell them online. Try to recycle items that are too damaged to donate.

✓ **Do** repurpose woven baskets, metal boxes, and other unused items at home for grouping similar items.

✗ **Don't** bite off more than you can chew. Organizing for an entire day with no break is a recipe for burnout.

✗ **Don't** dump donations at your local thrift shop before researching what items they accept—they might send your pile to the landfill.

✗ **Don't** start by buying a bunch of organizing supplies—you might not need them after you're done purging.

## ADDITIONAL TIPS FOR ZERO-WASTE HOME MAINTENANCE

Check salvage yards, Craigslist, Facebook Marketplace, and Nextdoor for building supplies.

Borrow home and garden tools from a tool-lending library.

Replace burnt out lightbulbs with energy-efficient LEDs.

Switch from single-use to rechargeable batteries.

Collect water from the shower and sink in a bucket to hydrate plants.

Contact DMA Choice and catalog companies to cancel junk mail.

Switch to paperless bills.

Swap print newspaper and magazine deliveries for digital versions.

Plug electronics into a power strip and flip the switch off when not in use.

Turn off lights when you leave a room.

Adjust the thermostat to reduce your use of heating or air conditioning, especially when you're away from home.

Open windows at night during summer to fill your home with cool air.

# Plastic-Free(ish) Action Plan

| SMALL WINS | BIG WINS |
|---|---|
| • Compost used paper towels.<br><br>• Make your own All-Purpose Cleaner (page 97).<br><br>• Switch to a biodegradable dish soap.<br><br>• Aim for a full washing machine for each load to reduce water and energy use.<br><br>• Return dry cleaning hangers and recycle plastic bags at a soft plastics drop-off. | • Swap paper towels for cloth rags.<br><br>• Make your own laundry detergent from bulk ingredients.<br><br>• Wash dishes with bar soap or a liquid bought in bulk.<br><br>• Skip the dryer and air-dry laundered garments instead. Use sunshine for natural stain removal.<br><br>• Request a reusable garment bag for dry cleaning or provide your own. |

# BABIES AND PETS

Parenting is hard. We go into it with big ideas about the type of parent we'll be; how we'll nurture, discipline, and nourish our children; and how we'll teach them right from wrong. Then, they're born and we just have to surrender to the very wild ride that parenting is.

When my husband and I planned for the birth of our son, we fully intended to continue our minimal, low-waste lifestyle. But it seemed like everywhere we turned people warned us, "Good luck keeping plastic out of your home (*not*)." I would vow to my husband (as many nonparents do), "We'll be different; *our* kid will be different." The truth was, I didn't really know what to expect as a first-time mom—what were the *must haves* and the *do withouts*? I consulted numerous parent friends, did extensive online research, and tried to be discerning, but still, plastic and baby clutter snuck into our carefully curated home.

And then, *he* was born. And I was tired (*so* tired), and hormonal (*so* hormonal), and overwhelmed . . . and did I mention tired? I found myself late-night shopping for sleep-inducing gadgets and garments while I desperately lulled my wide-eyed son to sleep. And, there were numerous gifts from thoughtful, well-meaning neighbors, friends, and relatives who "just couldn't resist!" Our once-empty trash can was starting to fill and baby things were everywhere.

With time (and sleep) we found a rhythm. We discovered the essentials our baby needed, which were way fewer than we prepared for, and sold or donated the rest. And, we've returned to minimalism and plastic-free living with renewed faith—it's been our saving grace for coping with the stress and chaos of parenthood. We're still figuring out what works and what doesn't and our household waste as a family of three is greater than it was as a household of two (plus a dachshund), but we're getting back to where we'd like to be.

If you want to stay minimal and plastic free as a parent, it's absolutely possible(*ish*). Do your research and be prepared, but also be gentle and kind to yourself while you figure out this whole parenting thing. Being a parent, especially a first-time parent, is incredibly hard, made even more challenging by societal pressure and judgment about what *good* parenting looks like. My hope is that you'll take my suggestions with a grain of salt, keep what works for your lifestyle, and just cut yourself a freaking break.

# Plastic-Free(ish) Baby Registry Checklist

Getting prepared for a tiny human you've never met can be challenging. If you ask for advice from any parent, they will offer a long list of recommendations. What you actually need will depend on your baby, lifestyle, and living space. I'm not saying you won't be tempted to purchase a fancy sound machine and five different styles of sleep sacks (all of which we did), but try to hold off buying most items until you've had time to adjust to this whole parenting thing. I've compiled a list of minimal essentials we used for the first six months and made some suggestions for items to hold off on or skip altogether. I also recommend trying to borrow or buy secondhand whenever possible to save money and minimize waste.

## SLEEPING

Baby monitor (or keep an ear out)

Bassinet (or Moses basket or co-sleep)

White noise machine (or play some peaceful music)

## GROOMING

Baby nail clippers

Natural rubber bath mat

Soap (try a gentle bar soap or liquid Castile)

Wood hairbrush with natural bristles

## CLOTH DIAPERING

20 to 30 cloth diapers (test a variety of styles before purchasing a full set)

30 to 40 cloth wipes

Changing mat (a bath towel or washable underpad also works)

Diaper cream (in a recyclable container or make your own)

Diaper pail with reusable liner (big enough to hold a two-day supply)

Diaper spray hose (attached to toilet or shower for rinsing soiled diapers)

Wet bag (for soiled diapers on the go)

Wipe warmer (or place wipes in a reusable container)

CONTINUED

WELCOME

## CLOTHING
## (WILL VARY BASED ON CLIMATE)

1 beanie

1 jacket or sweater

1 pair cloth booties

1 sun hat or bonnet

2 bottoms (pants or shorts)

2 sleep sacks

2 swaddle blankets

2 pairs of socks

4 onesies (long or short sleeves)

6 pajamas (footed for cold climates)

## FEEDING

2 cloth or silicone bibs or bandanas

Breastfeeding pillow (or a regular pillow)

Breast pump (rent from your hospital)

Glass or silicone bottle (borrow a variety of styles from friends or family to figure out what your baby prefers)

Rocking chair or glider (something comfortable; you'll be spending a *lot* of time in it)

Silicone bags (for storing and thawing frozen milk cubes)

Silicone or stainless steel ice cube tray (for freezing breast milk)

## TRANSPORTATION

Baby carrier (something structured and supportive for longer walks and hikes)

Baby wrap (something cloth and comfortable for babywearing around the house)

Car seat (a must if you're doing a hospital birth; they won't let you leave the facility without one)

## HOLD OFF

Crib (you might decide to co-sleep or do a Montessori-style floor bed instead)

High chair (you won't need one until your child is sitting up on their own and eating solid foods, around six months, or you might opt for a weaning table instead). We like the Stokke high chair because it's adjustable and can be modified as our son grows.

Stroller (we carried our baby everywhere until he was six months old)

Toys (repurpose cloth handkerchiefs and lightweight kitchen tools like silicone muffin cups instead)

## DO WITHOUT

Activity table (place the baby on a mat or towel on the ground so they can move freely)

Baby bathtub (used for a short period; place a rubber bath mat on the floor of the tub or kitchen sink instead)

Baby floor seat (puts baby in an unsupported position before they are ready)

Baby food maker

Baby laundry detergent (use regular detergent free from fragrance and dyes)

Baby towels and washcloths (use full-size towels you already have)

Bottle drying rack (use your dish rack)

Bottle sterilizer (use hot water and soap or run it through the dishwasher)

Bottle warmer (warm milk or bottle in hot water instead)

Bouncer and baby swing (same as activity table)

Burp cloths (use swaddle blankets instead)

Diaper bag (repurpose a large tote)

Mobile (do without or hang artwork on walls instead)

Nursing clothes and covers (drape a muslin blanket over your shoulder or breastfeed openly)

Plastic plate (use ceramic, enamel, or wood instead)

Play gym (place baby on a towel or mat on the floor with two or three simple toys)

Shoes (they won't need them until they can walk)

Sippy cup (use a glass or stainless-steel tumbler)

Walker (puts baby in an unsupported position before they are ready)

# Postpartum

Nothing really prepares you for giving birth, or the postpartum period. Our bodies go through an incredible transformation and it can take time to heal both physically and emotionally. I believe in prioritizing balance and self-care during this sensitive period, even if it means creating a little waste in the process. That said, there are a few ways to help you get through postpartum a little more sustainably.

**Nipple balm.** The first few weeks of breastfeeding can be a challenging adjustment complicated by engorgement and latch issues. Try moisturizing and soothing sensitive nips with a natural balm. I like Motherlove nipple cream, which comes in a glass jar, and Fat and the Moon nipple salve in a metal tin. They're both made from all-natural ingredients with no petroleum, so you won't have to rinse it off before breastfeeding.

**Reusable pads.** Whether you have a vaginal birth or C-section, you might experience some bleeding up to eight weeks after giving birth. Try reusable menstrual pads or menstrual underwear (see page 85) instead of disposable pads. They're absorbent, reusable, and feel much nicer against sensitive skin. I recommend having ten to twelve to last two to three days before needing to do laundry. Add a healing spray of one part aloe vera and one part witch hazel and spritz your pad or undies before wearing.

**Reusable nursing pads.** Deciding whether to breastfeed is a personal decision and can often be out of our control. If you do breastfeed, one item I found indispensable was reusable nursing pads to absorb leaking milk. The pads are made from cotton and flannel and are a much softer alternative to disposable pads. I recommend having three pairs.

# Diapers

Here is my take on cloth diapers. I've used cloth diapers since my son was born (he's now approaching two) and they've been great for our family, but they're not for everyone. They're obviously better for the planet; they don't contain any hidden chemicals or harsh fragrances; and they're cheaper than disposables over the long run. On the flip side, cloth diapers can be bulkier than disposables and need to be changed more frequently, and of course, there's extra laundry. I'm not going to say you must choose cloth diapers—it really depends on your schedule, access to a washing machine, and overall support network—but I will offer some information and tips to help you decide if it's the right path for your family.

# Check Out My Zero-Waste Diaper Bag

1. An assortment of **cloth diapers** and **hemp inserts**. I've found that all-in-ones are most similar in style to a disposable diaper and convenient for changes on the go.

2. Keep **cloth baby wipes** in a stainless-steel container, soaked in a homemade diaper solution (page 133). You could also bring dry wipes with a small spray bottle of solution.

3. A natural **diaper cream** in a recyclable metal tin.

4. A **muslin blanket** can be used as a diaper-changing mat, nursing cover, or burp cloth.

5. Skip purchasing a special diaper bag and repurpose a large purse or cloth tote to carry supplies.

6. Store soiled diapers and wipes in a **cloth wet bag**.

7. Give your baby a **wood teething ring** for playtime and soothing sore gums.

## TYPES OF CLOTH DIAPERS

Before you commit to cloth diapers, I recommend testing a range of styles and, ideally, borrowing them from a friend or purchasing secondhand. If you decide to continue, you'll need a two-day supply (about 20) before they need to be washed.

**All-in-ones.** All-in-ones (AIO) are most comparable to disposable diapers. They come in a diaper shape with a set of absorbent layers sewn inside and a built-in waterproof cover. They are convenient for quick changes and can be paired with a cloth insert for extra absorbency. The main disadvantages are they can take a long time to dry and can be expensive. We bought a set of AIOs secondhand and found this style the most helpful for quick changes when our son got more mobile.

**Fitted.** Fitted diapers are similar in shape to a disposable diaper but they feature elastic around the legs and are secured with hook-and-loop closures or snap fasteners. The diaper is usually made from cotton, bamboo, or hemp and paired with a waterproof cover. Compared to prefolds, fitted diapers are easier to put on—there's no complicated folding or fiddly fasteners, you just snap or fasten them into place. The negatives are that they require two separate layers and are one of the more expensive options. We started out with fitted diapers and they're one of my favorite diaper styles.

**Pocket.** The pocket diaper comes in a diaper shape with a built-in waterproof cover and snaps or hook-and-loop closures. They are usually made from polyester and feature a pocket into which you insert an absorbent pad. The main advantages of pocket diapers are they are fitted, easy to put on, and don't require a separate waterproof cover. You have to remove the pad from the pocket after they're used (before they go into the wash) which can get messy, and for that reason, they are one of my least favorite styles of cloth diapers.

**Prefolds.** Prefold diapers are the old-school cloth diaper trusted for decades. They feature a flat, rectangular cotton cloth that you fold into a diaper shape, secure with a fastener, and protect with a waterproof diaper cover. The advantages of prefolds are that they are inexpensive, versatile, and easy to clean. The disadvantages are that it can take some practice to get the folding right and they require two separate layers, which can be bulky.

# CLOTH DIAPER BENEFITS

**Cost savings.** It's estimated you'll spend anywhere from $1,200 to $2,500 (for premium options) on disposable diapers over the course of potty training. Cloth diapers cost more up front ($20 to $30 per diaper), but are a lot less expensive if you buy them secondhand and use them for subsequent children. They also have great resale value.

**Environmental savings.** Disposable diapers are a composite made from plastic and paper. Once they're used, they're trash—the materials cannot be separated. Cloth diapers are long lasting and reusable, but require a lot of laundry (and water and energy) to keep them clean. However, it's a lower carbon footprint compared to the water and energy used to create a brand new diaper from virgin materials.

**Health benefits.** Most disposable diapers are bleached with dioxin, a suspected carcinogen, and contain sodium polyacrylate, an absorbent gelling material that can cause skin irritation such as diaper rash. Cloth diapers don't contain chemicals and are typically made from cotton, hemp, or bamboo, which allow skin to breathe.

## CLOTH DIAPER CARE

If your baby is exclusively breastfed and not eating solid foods, you can put their soiled diapers straight into the diaper pail without rinsing. Once your baby is eating solids, you put #1 diapers straight into your pail and rinse #2 diapers over the toilet with a spray attachment—this is called the dry-pail method. You could also try the wet-pail method, where you soak diapers in a pail partially filled with water. Whatever method you choose, the diapers should be machine washed in hot water every two days, and air-drying is recommended to protect the fabric and shape. Also, sunshine is the best stain remover and sanitizer—I've found it much more effective than bleach.

## OTHER OPTIONS

**Biodegradable diapers.** Some brands offer biodegradable or compostable diapers, which are good alternatives to cloth diapers. However, most municipalities won't accept them in your curbside compost bin and it's unlikely they will break down in landfill. The most eco-friendly option is to use a service that picks up soiled diapers and composts them for you at a designated facility.

**Cloth diaper service.** If you choose the cloth diaper route but don't want to deal with the laundry, try a cloth diapering service. They deliver fresh cloth diapers and wipes each week and pick up the soiled ones.

**Elimination communication.** Another popular method for reducing diapering waste is elimination communication (EC), a practice in which a caregiver uses timing and signals to respond to a baby's elimination needs. From an early age, the caregiver pays attention to the baby's cues and enables them to pee or poop in a potty. Check out *Go Diaper Free* by Andrea Olson to learn more.

---

# CLOTH DIAPERS: DOS AND DON'TS

✓ **Do** borrow or buy cloth diapers secondhand; it's perfectly sanitary and a great way to reduce waste and save money.

✓ **Do** test a variety of styles and brands before you purchase a complete set.

✓ **Do** try a diaper service if you're looking for an eco-friendly alternative to washing cloth diapers at home.

✗ **Don't** invest in a set of brand-new cloth diapers—it will be a waste of money if you decide cloth diapers aren't for you.

✗ **Don't** commit to one style when you're starting out—you won't know what you like until you test a variety.

✗ **Don't** place compostable diapers in the green bin or toss them in your garden compost. They have to be processed at a designated facility.

# DIAPERING TOOLS

**Changing pad.** One of my few new baby purchases was the prettiest handwoven basket for diaper changes . . . that was never used. Instead, I found it easiest to diaper our son on a reusable underpad or towel laid on the floor. It gave me peace of mind knowing he couldn't roll off the dresser and it's been great for accommodating an increasingly mobile and wiggly toddler. I recommend having two on hand so you have one available while the other is being washed.

**Cloth baby wipes.** Commercial baby wipes are often made from synthetic materials and contain chemicals and fragrance that can irritate baby's bottom. Cloth wipes are not only reusable, they're also softer, more durable, and more absorbent than disposables. We soak our cloth wipes in a homemade solution (see Cloth Baby Wipes, opposite) before folding and storing them in a wipes warmer. Although a wipes warmer is made from plastic and isn't a necessity, I do think it can create a nicer diapering experience for both baby and parent. Another option is to skip the warmer and store the wipes in a reusable glass or stainless-steel container.

**Diaper pail (and liner).** You'll need a pail big enough to hold a two-day supply of diapers. We used a stainless-steel bin from Ubbi at first, which was great at containing smells, but discovered it was way too small and did not hold more than a couple bulky cloth diapers (most bins are designed for compact disposables). We sold our Ubbi and switched to a plastic Dekor pail with a reusable cloth liner. I'd love to see a stainless-steel bin option that's big enough to hold a few days' supply of cloth diapers.

# Cloth Baby Wipes

We've used cloth baby wipes for diaper changes since the day our son was born—and have learned a lot along the way. We started out by running the wipes under warm water, but discovered that water alone didn't work well for messier changes and the friction irritated his bottom. After some research, I discovered that baby wipes need two ingredients to be both effective and gentle: a mild soap, such as Castile, and a natural oil. You can also add a few drops of lavender or tea tree essential oil—both have antifungal properties that help prevent diaper rash, but first test the solution on a small patch of skin to make sure it doesn't cause further irritation.

**MAKES 30 TO 40 WIPES**

**INGREDIENTS**

2 teaspoons Castile soap (or other gentle soap)

2 teaspoons olive oil

10 drops tea tree essential oil or lavender essential oil (optional)

**SUPPLIES**

30 to 40 soft cloth wipes

Large bowl

Wipe warmer or other container

1. Place the wipes in a large bowl in the sink.

2. Fill the bowl with hot water and add the liquid soap while the water is running. You could also place bar soap directly into the bowl and let the water wash over it.

3. Drizzle in the olive oil and essential oil (if using).

4. Squeeze and roll each wipe to saturate, then remove excess liquid.

5. Place the folded wipes in a wipe warmer or other container of choice.

MILK

# Babies and Toddlers

**Bathing and grooming.** Most baby shampoos and soaps come packaged in wasteful plastic bottles and contain artificial fragrances that can irritate sensitive skin. To bathe baby head to toe without chemicals or plastic waste, try liquid Castile soap bought in bulk or a natural bar soap. And, skip the plastic baby tub—they're short-lived and you can just as easily bathe baby in the kitchen sink or bathtub on top of a towel or natural rubber mat (I like one made by Hevea Planet) in an inch or two of water.

For grooming fine baby hair, use a wood hairbrush with soft natural bristles. If cradle cap is an issue, massage some olive oil into the scalp while bathing baby and use the brush to gently exfoliate and remove flakes. To dry baby, use a regular bath towel. Tiny towels are cute, but an adult towel works just as well.

**Clothing.** Who doesn't love tiny clothes? Delicate dresses with ruffles, petite linen pants, and miniature high-tops are all adorable—and generally impractical. Kids wear out clothes fast, especially during the first year. What fits one week will be too snug the next, and there are inevitable stains and holes as they become more mobile and start eating solid foods. Most clothes we bought for our son prior to birth didn't end up being used because they were the wrong size or too fiddly to dress him in. Luckily, we purchased most of his clothing secondhand and inherited many others from friends and family. My biggest recommendation with kids' clothes at any age is to buy them secondhand. Stick to garments made from cotton and other natural fabrics that allow their skin to breathe and encourage free movement, and don't bother with shoes until they're actually walking. Donate, sell, or give away anything you don't use.

**Toys.** In our home, we've tried to cultivate Montessori and RIE (Resources for Infant Educarers) parenting traditions by selecting simple, open-ended toys made from sustainable materials such as wood, cloth, silicone, and metal. Toys that are baby operated versus battery operated help promote creativity and encourage children to develop their sense of touch and texture. Whereas most plastic toys are trash once they break, wooden and cloth toys are long lasting and, ultimately, biodegradable (they're also much nicer to look at). We limit the selection so our home isn't taken over, and store a few extra to rotate in every couple of months. I recommend buying toys secondhand or not at all because, chances are, you will likely receive more as gifts than you actually need. And, most often, your kid will forgo all your beautiful, carefully selected toys for a cardboard box. *Kids*. Go figure.

**Meals.** Witnessing a baby eat their first foods can be an exciting and messy time. We want our kids to get off to a good start and recognize that early nutrition can help lay the groundwork for healthy eating habits throughout life. When the time came to introduce solid foods to our son, we decided to try baby-led weaning. With baby-led weaning, you skip the purees and mashes and feed your child steamed or roasted vegetables, soft fruits, oatmeal, pancakes, pasta, and any other soft food they can easily grasp in their hands and bring to their mouth (it has nothing to do with weaning from breastfeeding, just to be clear). The benefits of baby-led weaning are that the child eats the same foods you eat (no extra cooking) and you don't have to spoon puree patiently into their tiny mouth. Rather, you present your baby with a few options and they decide what they want to eat and how much. It also helps prevent food waste and eliminates the need to purchase purees in jars and plastic squeeze pouches. I love that baby-led weaning makes meals simple and fosters independence, and our dachshund loves to eat the food dropped on the floor. Check out *Baby-Led Weaning* by Gill Rapley and Tracey Murkett to learn more.

# MEALTIME TOOLS

Skip the plastic bowl and cup and start 'em young with reusable alternatives. Using real, breakable tableware can help children develop their sense of control and learn responsibility. Maybe just don't use your favorite ceramics.

**Cup.** A plastic sippy cup can prevent spills and make for a tidier home. However, prolonged use can be bad for baby teeth and lead to orthodontic issues. Skip the sippy and use a durable glass jam jar or stainless-steel tumbler. They'll get the hang of it in no time.

**Cutlery.** We have a small set of stainless-steel utensils for our son that we introduced early on. At first, they were dumped on the floor or used as tiny percussion instruments, but with time and practice, he started to use them with confidence.

**Plate.** Babies can be unpredictable. What they love to eat one day may end up dumped on the floor the next. You could go the Montessori route and use a real ceramic plate from the start. If you're concerned about breakability, use an enamel or wood plate instead.

# Check Out My Zero-Waste Play Area

1.  **Limit selection.** Displaying five or six toys at a time on the toy shelf promotes a peaceful, tidy environment. Keep a few extras in storage to rotate in every couple of months.

2.  **Make it accessible.** The toy shelf is low and open so our son can select what he wants to play with and, ideally, put it away when he's done (still working on that).

3.  **Group like items.** Toys are grouped by category so our son knows where to find them. Loose blocks are stored in one basket and wooden train tracks are stored in another.

4.  **Keep it natural.** Open-ended toys made from natural materials such as wood and cloth help promote creativity and develop the sense of touch and texture.

# Big Kids

It's said that kids are like sponges, and even before they can talk, they notice the way we interact with our peers and the world around us. I once read that the best way to ensure your child turns into a kind adult is to model kind behavior. If our children notice we treat our family, friends, and the environment with care, they will be more likely to do the same. Older children love to be given responsibility and can become active participants in a waste-free lifestyle, whether picking out their own snacks and treats from the bulk section or composting food scraps after meals. Here are a few additional tips to get them involved early on.

1. **Practice minimalism.** People often complain that kids come with a lot of clutter, including school projects and toys littering the home. When it comes to toys, practice a one-in, one-out rule—cultivate quality over quantity and let them decide which toys they are ready to part with before adding something new to the rotation. This practice can be especially helpful for birthdays and holidays. Request that well-meaning family and friends give the gift of experiences, or offer concrete suggestions on what types of sustainable toys you are in the market for.

2. **Simplify parties.** There's a lot of pressure on parents to plan elaborate kids' parties, complete with entertainment, dazzling decorations, and cute party favors. Keep it simple with easy-to-eat finger foods (remember, pizza boxes are compostable) and serve everything on real plates, or enamel plates if you're worried about breakage. Have one simple birthday banner that can be reused every year and adorned with homemade or borrowed decorations. Ditch balloons, which are short-lived and can pose a hazard to wildlife when they end up in the environment. Host the festivities outdoors at a park with a playground for easy entertainment. Skip the party favors and send guests home with an extra slice of cake in recycled containers.

3. **Plan for school.** Kids come home from school with a lot of paper and projects. Talk to teachers at the beginning of the year to see how you can limit the quantity of paper coming into your home. Request that assignments be sent digitally when possible. For school supplies, consider sustainable options—beeswax crayons, refillable pens and pencils, high-lighter pencils, and cardboard binders and composition

books made from recycled paper. Buy backpacks second-hand or made from natural or recycled materials. For projects, encourage reusing materials that would otherwise end up in the recycling bin, such as toilet paper tubes, egg cartons, and glass condiment jars.

4.  **Always buy secondhand (or borrow).** Between clothing, shoes, toys, school supplies, food, and extracurricular activities, kids can be expensive. Shop at consignment shops or buy-sell-trade groups online for affordable clothing, toys, and sports equipment and bring kids to the thrift store to help pick out purchases. Go to the library to check out books and rent movies. You could also host a toy and clothing swap with parent friends to refresh a wardrobe and toy shelf.

5.  **Encourage active participation.** Kids love responsibility and feeling like they make a meaningful contribution to daily life. Take them grocery shopping and let them help fill glass jars and cloth bags with bulk items. Start a compost at home and show them how this nutrient-rich soil enriches the garden. Encourage them to spend time in nature and make a game out of litter cleanup. Learning about environmental responsibility from an early age will help instill the importance in caring for Earth as they mature.

# Check Out My Kid's Zero-Waste Backpack

1. This Fjallraven **backpack,** purchased secondhand, is made from recycled polyester and organic cotton.

2. The **decomposition book** is made from post-consumer recycled paper and metal wire.

3. This **stainless-steel ballpoint pen** is refillable and recyclable. The Sprout **wood pencil** contains a seed capsule that can be planted at the pencil's end of life. The pencil nub can be used as a garden marker.

4. The **metal ruler** is durable and long lasting.

5. This Stabilo 3-in-1 pencil can be used as a **highlighter.**

6. Dust from the **natural gum eraser** can be composted.

7. This **brass pencil sharpener** is long-lasting and recyclable.

# Kid's Zero-Waste Lunch Kit

I believe it's important to encourage good habits for children early on, whether eating healthy, taking care of belongings, or respecting the environment. Using reusables may not seem as convenient or practical as disposable lunch supplies, but it does give children responsibility and allows them to participate in waste reduction. If you're worried about belongings getting lost, label them with a name and contact info.

## THE ESSENTIALS

1. **Bamboo utensils.** This bamboo spork is lightweight and handy for waste-free dining on the go. Or, just wrap cutlery from home in a cloth napkin.

2. **Cloth napkin.** A cloth napkin is handy for cleaning little hands, wiping noses, and mopping up spills, or pack an unpaper towel.

3. **Lunch bag or box.** (Not pictured.) Skip single-use paper bags and pack lunches in a reusable bag or a retro metal lunchbox.

4. **Reusable water bottle.** Start good hydration (and environmental) habits with a stainless-steel or glass water bottle that can be refilled at the water fountain.

5. **Stainless-steel lunchbox.** You'll want a lunchbox that's easy to open and can hold a full meal without being bulky. I like this PlanetBox container with divided compartments.

## THE EXTRAS

6. **Insulated container.** This will come in handy if you want to pack a hot meal, like soup, or keep perishable foods, like yogurt, cool.

7. **Silicone sandwich bag.** A sustainable alternative to disposable sandwich and snack bags that's easy to open and won't leak.

# Pets

From partners to children to roommates, it's important to get your whole household on board with zero-waste living to make the biggest impact on waste reduction. Pets (or fur babies) are an essential part of the family and can help contribute to your zero-waste goals. Like all areas of plastic-free living, the easiest way to start is to practice minimalism. Does your dog need ten different chew toys, or one or two high-quality options made from natural materials? Does your cat require a sprawling cat condo with scratch posts in every room, or would they be just as happy with a cozy nook with natural bedding and a homemade scratch pad made from recycled cardboard?

If you don't have a pet but are thinking about adding one to the family, it's worth mentioning there is an abundance of wonderful animals in shelters looking for homes. Adopting an animal from a shelter frees space and resources so more animals can be rescued, and takes business away from puppy mills, which have a bad reputation for their unethical treatment of animals. We vote with our wallets so remember to adopt, not shop.

# 5 Zero-Waste Tips for (Fur) Babies

From basics like kibble and poo bags to custom accessories and fancy shampoos, pets can create a surprising amount of waste. Here are a few tips to keep your furry family members happy, healthy, and low waste.

1. **Food.** Some pet food stores offer dry kibble in bulk. If you can't find bulk options, buy the biggest bag available or purchase wet food in recyclable cans. Open Farm and Wellness Core have a program with TerraCycle that accepts mailed-in empty packaging for recycling. We also add leftover table scraps to supplement the kibble and make it stretch longer—mostly plain foods without lots of seasoning, like blueberries, apple, oatmeal, and roasted veggies. Many stores also offer package-free treats you can buy with your own cloth bag, or you can find a recipe to make your own. Please note that it's always a good idea to consult your veterinarian before making any changes to your pet's diet.

2. **Toys.** Pet toys endure a lot of wear and tear. Buy something made from natural materials like a hemp rope or wool mouse, which are often more durable and longer lasting. Also, if the toy is torn apart, you'll have peace of mind knowing your pet is not consuming any synthetic materials. Our dog's favorite toy is a hemp duck stuffed with wool from Honest Pet Products—it's lasted many years, despite lots of playing and chewing, and can be composted if it eventually becomes too worn. We also love Kong, a weighted toy made from natural rubber that can be filled with kibble and treats.

3. **Grooming.** To bathe your dog, use Castile soap or a bar soap. Chagrin Valley makes one with cedarwood and lavender that repels fleas and ticks naturally (and can even be used on humans to deter insects while camping!). Cats naturally groom themselves and do not need to be washed with soap. For both cats and dogs, use a wood brush with wood or metal bristles and be sure to compost the fur when you're done.

4. **Waste.** Pet waste cannot be added to your garden compost or green bin. Some cities allow you to flush dog waste down the toilet (just the poop, not the bag), but you'll have to check with your local water treatment facility. Cat feces should never be flushed because they contain pathogens and parasites that can contaminate the water supply. If you have outdoor space, you could try a DIY pet poo worm farm, but note that the castings should only be added to ornamental plants, not your vegetable garden. The next best thing is biodegradable pet poo bags, paper bags, or newspaper but note that even "compostable" pet bags are unlikely to break down in landfill without proper access to sunlight and oxygen. For cats, skip the plastic liner and choose compostable litter made from recycled newspaper, sawdust, or natural pellets and dispose of it in the trash in a sealed paper bag. Waste and sawdust from rabbit, hamster, and guinea pig cages can be composted.

5. **Accessories.** Look for leashes and collars secondhand, or if you're buying new, favor natural materials like cotton, hemp, and leather. Choose metal or ceramic bowls for food and water—they're long lasting and easy to clean. Donate any unused accessories in good condition to your local animal shelter.

## You Can Compost That

- Baby hair

- Baby nail clippings

- Cloth diaper pads
(at the end of their useful life)

- Cloth wipes
(at the end of their useful life)

- Compostable diapers
(through a designated
service only)

- Compostable wipes
(made from 100 percent
natural materials)

- Dog nail clippings

- Natural pet toys
(made from cotton, hemp,
wool, etc.)

- Pet accessories
(made from natural materials)

- Pet fur

- Pet poo
(in a DIY pet poo worm bin)

# Plastic-Free(ish) Action Plan

| SMALL WINS | BIG WINS |
|---|---|
| • Ditch disposable diapers and try a compostable diaper service.<br><br>• Swap synthetic baby wipes for a compostable version.<br><br>• Buy clothes and toys made from natural fabrics and sustainable materials.<br><br>• Buy pet food in the largest bag available to reduce packaging waste.<br><br>• Switch to compostable pet waste bags and cat litter. | • Use cloth diapers (bonus points for buying secondhand) or try elimination communication.<br><br>• Switch to cloth wipes soaked in a homemade solution (see page 133).<br><br>• Buy the majority of baby essentials secondhand or borrow them from friends and family.<br><br>• Buy bulk pet food and treats in cloth bags, or learn how to make your own.<br><br>• Start a pet poo worm bin in your backyard. |

So far we've looked at the many different ways to integrate zero-waste habits into your everyday routine. From groceries to food storage, clean beauty to cleaning up, and taking care of babies (children and pets). But what about the *nonessential* areas of our life? The purchases and activities that make us feel pampered, rejuvenated, and bring us joy? Things like treating ourselves to a new outfit, taking a vacation, getting outdoors, and throwing a party.

Some people will argue that to be truly eco-friendly you should simply practice restraint—don't buy new clothes, limit vacations to a small radius near home, and forgo gift exchanges for gift experiences. Although shopping, travel, and the holidays are all notoriously wasteful, there are ways to practice minimalism and reduce waste without living like a Spartan. The key is adapting the principles of zero waste to suit *your* needs and enhance your lifestyle.

It can take some trial and error to find the right balance between sustainability and self-care, but with time and patience, you'll find your sweet spot: zero-waste living will help simplify your schedule, save money, and add unexpected joy and beauty to your home. Let's explore how to curate your most fabulous wardrobe, take a relaxing vacation, spend some time in nature, and celebrate holidays and other special occasions without creating a mountain of waste in the process.

# Wardrobe

We've all bought *those* clothes. You know the ones—the glittery dress for New Year's Eve; the boho romper for an outdoor festival; the trendy Halloween costume with matching accessories. I'm referring to fast fashion. Clothes that are mass-produced, cheaply made, and designed to be disposed of *fast*. Fast fashion has become synonymous with everything that's wrong with the fashion industry, but what's really so bad about having access to affordable, trendy clothing?

It turns out, churning out clothes at discount prices comes at a huge environmental cost. Fast fashion is typically made from synthetic fabrics that can, literally, fall apart after a few wearings and end up in landfill. Also, the insatiable demand for low prices and quick turnaround leads to unethical labor practices including meager wages, child labor, and unsafe labor conditions. So, if you love fashion, but want to live more sustainably (and ethically), do you have to start crocheting your own sweaters from recycled yarn? You could, but you can also live your most fashionable and fabulous life, shop with integrity, *and* protect the environment without breaking the bank.

# Check Out My Zero-Waste Capsule Wardrobe

1. **Space it out.** Garments are evenly spaced on hangers so you can see everything at a glance.

2. **Stay neutral (maybe).** Curating mostly neutral colors makes it easy to mix and match pieces.

3. **Maximize space.** Small closet space is maximized with a hanging rack.

4. **Keep it natural.** Most garments are made from natural fabrics such as cotton, linen, and silk.

5. **Stow seasonals.** (Not pictured.) Seasonal items, like bulky winter coats, are stowed away to help save space.

6. **Add some flair.** A few curated accessories and vintage pieces help add texture and personality to your wardrobe.

**Buy fewer; buy better.** When clothing feels cheap and disposable, that's how we treat it. When we limit shopping and instead invest in a few quality pieces, we're more likely to take care of our wardrobe and make it last. Although good-quality products can cost more up front, they last much longer than fast fashion, so you don't have to replace them as often. Synthetic fabrics like polyester, acrylic, and nylon shed thousands of tiny plastic fibers that end up in the ocean and never biodegrade, so it's best to favor natural materials like cotton, silk, leather, hemp, linen, bamboo, and wool. Natural fabrics are also longer lasting and ultimately, biodegradable (you can even add the dryer lint to your compost pile).

**Curate your capsule.** How is it that we can have an overflowing closet and nothing to wear? When we have too many choices, we're more likely to get overwhelmed, forget what we have, and purchase duplicates. Reduce the amount of clothes, shoes, and accessories you have to create a capsule wardrobe—a curated selection of timeless, quality staples you can mix and match and wear often. Limiting your wardrobe to garments in which you feel comfortable and polished makes it easier to get dressed and can even amplify your personal style. Think daily uniform—you don't have to restrict yourself to neutrals or jeans and T-shirts. It's about finding what makes you feel confident—maybe that's pastels and florals.

**Vote with your wallet.** In a perfect world, we'd only buy second-hand clothes made from natural fabrics. The next best option is to vote with our wallets by supporting businesses that use sustainable and ethical manufacturing practices. Luckily, there are a growing number of brands and retailers stepping up to the plate. Some personal favorites are Christy Dawn for dresses made from recycled textiles, Girlfriend Collective for leggings and sports bras made from plastic bottles, and Patagonia for outdoor apparel made from recycled athletic gear.

**Care and repair.** Treat clothing with care whether that means hand washing or reducing washes so fabrics keep their shape and colors don't fade. You can also extend the life of garments by skipping the dryer to air-dry instead and learning to mend rips and tears. If sewing isn't your forte, find a tailor. Having a garment professionally tailored is also a great way to give clothes a new life, such as altering baggy trousers or hemming a long dress. For footwear, keep soles clean with an old toothbrush, baking soda, and dish soap and consider getting your worn-out boots polished and resoled by a cobbler—it's often cheaper than buying a new pair and more sustainable.

**Donate, sell, recycle.** Even though there are numerous ways to sell or donate clothes, 84 percent of unwanted textiles were sent to landfill in the United States in 2016 according to the US Environmental Protection Agency. Find a business or organization that accepts donations or host a clothing swap with friends. Lessen the guilt of parting with valuable or never-worn pieces by reselling them through a consignment shop or an online resale site. For the unsalvageable items with holes, rips, and stains beyond repair, repurpose what you can and find a store that recycles used textiles, like Goodwill and H&M. Shoes have to be in decent wearable condition to be donated, so if your sneakers are too beat up, your best bet is recycling. Nike's Reuse-A-Shoe program grinds down old athletic shoes (regardless of brand) and turns them into sports surfaces and new sneakers and apparel. For more tips, see my recycling guide on page 192.

# 5 Zero-Waste Tips for Thrift Shopping

*You there*, yes *you,* holding the synthetic pants! Put down that fast fashion and let me introduce you to a shop full of clothes that are anything but basic and say, "Hey world, I'm fabulous *and* sustainable!" I'm referring to thrift and consignment shops full of well-made, well-curated, and well-loved clothing, shoes, and accessories. Buying secondhand is similar to a treasure hunt—most stores are organized with little rhyme or reason and strike-outs can be common. But with time, patience, and a *little* luck, you'll discover great pieces that are timeless, sustainable, and one-of-a-kind (not to mention affordable). Here are a few more tips for striking gold at the thrift shop.

1. **Shop men's.** Ladies, this is a game changer. Don't limit your search to the women's section; be sure to check out the men's area. Some of my favorite vintage items are menswear—vintage T-shirts, bomber jackets, even Levi's jeans. I often prefer the boxy cut of men's shirts and the look of an oversized jacket.

2. **Bring a friend.** Thrifting takes patience and nothing helps pass the time like having a friend join you. Bring some-one who will give you the *honest* truth. Sometimes I can get carried away by the novelty of a piece, never mind if it actually fits, looks flattering, or is practical—am I really going to wear a silk trench coat if my daily uniform is jeans and a T-shirt? I'm looking for bru-tal honesty here, people! Plus, what's more fun than trying on quirky thrift finds with a partner in crime? Cue the montage.

3. **One-in, one-out rule.** Before you shop, take inventory of your closet and make some cuts. Make a pile of clothes to donate, sell, and recycle. Some stores even give you the option of cash or trade in exchange for your clothing and shoes. Just don't feel bad if they don't accept many items, or none at all. Each store has different requirements and their buying criteria will vary depending on the brand, season, material, and condition of the garment.

4. **Quality over quantity.** If you find something you like, pay attention to the quality of the piece. Look at the label to find out who made it, where it was made, and what it's made from. Look at the hardware: Are buttons missing? Does the zipper open and close? Are there any stains or holes? If you find an issue with the piece, be honest with yourself—how likely is it that you'll have it repaired? If you still want to buy it, ask the shopkeeper if they'll offer a discount (10 percent to 15 percent is standard for damaged items).

5. **Feel factor.** It's important to try before you buy when you thrift. For one, thrift stores rarely have a return policy. And second, it's important to feel the fabric against your skin. I used to buy pieces that looked great on the hanger, but felt too snug or scratchy for prolonged wear. If it's uncomfortable in the store, you're going to hate wearing it in the real world for hours at a time. If you're buying online, request measurements to compare to other pieces in your closet and stick to brands whose fit you know.

Don't forget to refuse the store receipt and bring a reusable bag to tote your treasures home.

# Zero-Waste Travel Kit

My favorite part about traveling is trying new foods. I always do extensive research before a trip and make a list of restaurants and markets to scope out. When we're home, my husband and I cook the majority of our meals—so travel gives us the opportunity to indulge in new flavors and sample local cuisine.

The hardest part about traveling is also the food, specifically finding healthy and sustainable options in the middle of an airport food desert. Nothing is worse than being tired, dehydrated, and hungry, surrounded by greasy, wasteful options. The best way to minimize trash during a long day of travel is to bring your own meals and snacks or plan to eat before the flight at a restaurant with real plates and cutlery. Here are a few essentials (and some extras) to help you pack meals and reduce waste on the go.

## THE ESSENTIALS

1. **Bamboo utensils.** A set of bamboo utensils is lightweight and essential for waste-free dining. You could also bring a regular metal fork and spoon, but skip the knife—it's not allowed in carry-ons and will be confiscated by security.

2. **Cloth napkin.** A cloth napkin helps keep things tidy and can multitask as a handkerchief, cleaning rag, or pastry carrier. When you get to your destination, hand wash it in the sink with soap and air-dry.

3. **Silicone sandwich bag.** Refuse packaged foods offered inflight and bring bulk snacks like trail mix, fruit, veggies, granola, and chocolate (*obviously*). You could also use a silicone bag to pack a sandwich, or my favorite travel meal—leftover pizza.

4. **Reusable container.** If traveling makes you hungry, bring a nourishing meal in a reusable container. It will also come in handy at your destination—to pack meals for day trips, use when ordering street food, and store leftovers.

5. **Water bottle.** Always empty your bottle before entering the security line, then beeline to the nearest water fountain. Skip the plastic cup onboard and request refills in your bottle. Some airlines don't allow this, so try to bring a bottle large enough to keep you hydrated for long flights.

## THE EXTRAS

6. **Reusable coffee cup.** If you require lots of water *and* caffeine to get through a long day of travel, ask for coffee or tea to go in a reusable coffee cup. Or skip it and ask for beverages in your empty water bottle.

7. **Reusable straw.** Remember to bring a glass or stainless-steel straw if you plan to drink lots of smoothies, milkshakes, or piña coladas at your destination. Hey, it's a vacation—*treat yourself!*

8. **Reusable tote and produce bags.** If you're staying somewhere that has a kitchen, don't forget to bring a tote and reusable produce bags for low-waste groceries.

# 5 Tips for Plastic-Free(ish) Travel

The most eco-friendly way to vacation would be to skip air travel and take a nearby road trip instead. But even when you arrive at your destination, there will be challenges ready to derail your zero-waste progress. Does the hotel in which you're staying recycle and compost? Does the city you're visiting have the waste infrastructure to process either? I'll tell you what isn't fun—being on vacation and spending the whole time worrying about trash.

We can get thrown off our routines when we travel, whether that be diet, exercise, or waste reduction. You can go the extra mile and pack all your recyclables in your luggage so you can properly dispose of them at home, or you can accept that you won't be able to control every piece of garbage you create on vacation, despite your best efforts. Here are some ways to be mindful about waste reduction on vacation, without letting it take over the trip.

1.  **Pack light.** I know, you *finally* have a reason to wear all the fabulous clothes you don't wear on the regular. But packing light and, ideally, fitting everything into one carry-on bag can help reduce carbon emissions from the plane. Although most of the plane's weight comes from its infrastructure, we can all help lighten the load. Try to stick with neutral, versatile clothes and wear any bulky layers or boots onboard. Also, bringing a carry-on versus checking a bag means no plastic luggage tag (trash) or waiting for your bag to arrive at the carousel (as much fun as that is).

2.  **Refuse airline freebies.** Download your boarding pass onto your phone so you won't need a printed ticket. On the plane say, "no, thanks" to plastic packaged snacks and disposable cups by bringing your own food and water. Ask for the entire can of seltzer and check to see if the airline recycles or take it with you and recycle it when you land. Bring your own headphones and eye mask so you can refuse the disposable ones offered inflight. A warm jacket or thick scarf can double as a blanket or pillow.

3.  **BYO toiletries.** Resist those adorable complementary shampoos, sewing kits, and shower caps provided by the hotel. Don't even look at those plastic-wrapped cups and let housekeeping know you didn't touch them so they can be reused for the next guest. Instead, pack your own toiletries, like bar soap in a metal tin or bulk shampoo and body wash in reusable silicone travel tubes. I've never had an issue with packing full-size toothpaste, but you could bring some in a small jar or try toothpaste tablets.

4.  **Try a home stay.** Renting a home or apartment versus staying in a hotel is a great way to experience local culture and reduce waste. If you get a rental with a kitchen, you can cook some of your own low-waste meals; and check with your host to ensure there is recycling and composting. Hotels tend to waste energy and water, keeping lights on 24/7 and frequently washing linens and towels. If you do stay at a hotel, skip the housekeeping service or request they don't change sheets or towels.

5.  **Keep it local.** Do some research before you travel to see what bulk options are available. Find a farmers' market, natural foods store, or bodega for local and seasonal foods. Eat at restaurants that cultivate local ingredients. Buy coffee from cafes that roast their own beans. Sample street foods—it's a great way to support the local economy and try local ingredients and spices. To me, the best souvenirs are memories from amazing meals (and maybe some treats or spices bought in bulk).

# Check Out My Zero-Waste Suitcase

1. Make your own travel-sized toiletries by decanting them into reusable **silicone tubes** or **glass bottles**. Everything is stored in a leak-proof, transparent silicone bag.

2. Bring your own **headphones** for listening to music, podcasts, and in-flight entertainment so you can decline the disposable ones offered inflight.

3. Skip paper magazines and download books, podcasts, magazines, and movies onto your **smart device** or bring a lightweight paperback.

4. **Bar soaps** are great for travel—they're light, compact, and won't leak all over your bag. Protect your bar in a reusable metal tin.

5. Travel light with one **carry-on bag** to help reduce carbon emissions from the plane and skip the plastic luggage tag used for checked bags.

6. Bring a **stainless-steel tea infuser** and **loose-leaf tea** in a glass jar to avoid single-use tea bags at your destination.

7. A **large wool scarf** doubles as a blanket or pillow inflight.

# Kitchen Sink Granola

For travel snacks, I love to bring something sweet and salty that will boost my energy during a long day, without making me crash. Granola is easy to make and can be customized with any leftover nuts and seeds lying around in the pantry. Don't have maple syrup? Try agave. Ran out of olive oil? Sub coconut oil. The granola also makes a great homemade gift during the holidays—whip up a batch and pack it in a Mason jar.

**MAKES ABOUT 4½ CUPS**

## INGREDIENTS

3½ cups rolled oats

1½ cups mixed nuts, seeds, dried fruit, etc. (I like pecans, almonds, peanuts, sunflower seeds, coconut flakes, currants, and raisins)

½ teaspoon salt

½ cup maple syrup, agave, or honey

¼ cup olive oil, coconut oil, or avocado oil

## SUPPLIES

1 large bowl

1 sheet pan

1 silicone baking mat (optional) or parchment paper (compost when you're done)

1. Preheat the oven to 350°F.

2. In a large bowl, mix together the oats, nuts, seeds, and salt.

3. Stir in the maple syrup and olive oil until the oats and toppings are coated.

4. Spread the granola in an even layer on a sheet pan lined with a silicone baking mat or parchment paper.

5. Bake until golden and fragrant, 15 to 20 minutes. Stir halfway through to achieve an even color (optional).

6. Remove and let cool for 10 minutes, then consume or store in an airtight container at room temperature for up to 6 months.

# Outdoors

Spending time outdoors is a great way to connect with the mission of living zero waste and is an opportunity to put low-waste principles into action. And yet, being away from home without access to a stove, sink, or compost bucket can pose some obstacles to waste-reduction goals. The majority of this book focuses on how to be more sustainable at home, but a zero-waste lifestyle isn't put on pause when we step out the front door. Most often people will turn to the convenience of packaged goods that are light and easy to dispose of, such as plastic-wrapped granola bars, single-use plates, and plastic cutlery. But, wouldn't it be nice if we could enjoy nature while creating zero waste in the process? From hiking to picnics to overnight camping trips, you can spend quality time with Mother Nature without producing a mountain of waste in the process.

# Zero-Waste Picnic Kit

Food tastes better when you're outdoors, especially when you've worked up an appetite from hiking or swimming. Enjoy your meal alfresco and do Mother Nature a solid by leaving no trace behind. Reusables are not only better for the environment, but also add elegance to a simple, rustic meal, even when you're sitting on the ground.

## THE ESSENTIALS

1. **Basket.** Pick one with a flat bottom so food won't tip over and make a mess. A sturdy tote bag also works.

2. **Blanket.** I like to use a linen tablecloth or cotton towel that you can shake free of crumbs and toss in the wash.

3. **Cutlery.** Ditch flimsy plastic utensils and bring real cutlery from home. Besides, do plastic knives ever really work?

4. **Reusable plates.** Bring something durable and lightweight to eat on, like enamel plates, or skip them and pack finger foods.

5. **Knife.** Something foldable, like an Opinel pocketknife, so you don't accidentally slice a finger when reaching into the basket.

6. **Reusable tumblers.** These enamel mugs are multifunctional and hold everything from snacks to water to rosé. They're lighter than glass and won't break if you knock one over.

## THE EXTRAS

7. **Wood cutting board.** Perfect for assembling sandwiches or a cheese platter. Make it multitask by turning it into a serving board.

# 5 Zero-Waste Tips for Camping

Many years ago my husband and I took a three-month back-packing and road trip through the Pacific Northwest, and that experience became the catalyst for transitioning to a minimal, zero-waste lifestyle. I would be remiss not to cover tips for zero-waste camping. Truthfully, when we made our trip, we did produce waste (quite a bit, in fact). We were both fairly new to backpacking and just starting to learn about the plastic-free movement, but it was strange to spend two nights off the grid, bathing in alpine lakes and cooking meals over a propane stove, only to return home with a backpack full of garbage. We've learned a lot since then and have compiled some tips to help minimize your camping footprint.

1. **Borrow gear or buy it secondhand.** Backpacking gear is expensive, so the best thing to do, if you're just starting out, is to borrow as much as you can. Make sure you like the whole "sleeping outdoors" thing before you invest in a fancy sleeping bag or top-of-the-line tent. If you're into it, try to buy most of your gear secondhand. Believe me, there are tons of people who had big dreams of hiking the Pacific Crest Trail only to realize they hate going unshowered—you can score some good-quality gear that's practically new from Craigslist and Facebook Marketplace.

2. **Skip premade meals.** If you visit the camping section at any outdoors store, you'll find an array of dehydrated meals in shiny plastic pouches. Although these premade meals are light and compact, and offer convenience after a long day of hiking, you can just as easily pack your own food (it will also taste a million times better than dehydrated "pad thai"). Stick to easy-to-prepare foods bought in bulk, such as oats, quinoa, and dried pasta and high-energy snacks like trail mix, granola, and dried fruit. Wash and prep fresh produce before you go and keep in mind which foods are most perishable and need to be consumed first. Also, remember that anything you bring needs to be packed out, including food scraps, so plan ahead.

3. **Remember reusables.** In terms of packing meals, keep things as lightweight as possible. Skip heavy glass jars and stick to silicone sandwich bags and beeswax wraps. Don't forget cloth napkins, reusable cutlery, and water bottles. Although we usually prefer stainless-steel water bottles, we like to bring a set of BPA-free Nalgene bottles on trips because they weigh less and we don't mind if they get scuffed up on trails. We also bring a water purifier to fill our bottles with fresh drinking water from lakes and streams. Many backpacking camp stoves comes with a built-in pot you can eat out of, but you may want to bring a stainless-steel container, enamel plate, or collapsible silicone bowl for additional campers.

4. **Leave (most) toiletries behind.** The best way to leave no trace behind is to leave the majority of your toiletries at home. Some essentials you may want to consider are a bar of soap, sunscreen in a metal tin, bug repellent stick in a cardboard tube, toothpaste in a small container, bamboo toothbrush, and a menstrual cup. Check the ingredients of anything you plan to bring to make sure they are unscented and biodegradable so they won't harm water sources or wildlife.

5. **Pack out waste.** The goal for camping is to leave the grounds as clean (if not cleaner) than when you arrived. That includes everything from food packaging to leftover scraps from meals and even toilet paper. When you're planning to camp somewhere remote, without access to a bathroom, be sure to check local waste guidelines. Some places allow campers to dig a "cat hole" to do their business in whereas at high-elevation and in sensitive areas sometimes campers are asked to pack out solid human waste. For peeing, stay two hundred feet away from a water source and you can try the shake-dry method, or bring a reusable cloth to wash and dry at your campsite. Always be sure to wash hands with soap and water when you're done, or bring homemade hand sanitizer.

# Holidays and Entertaining

The holidays can be a wonderful time of year with family traditions, festive decorations, delicious home-cooked meals, and time to relax and recharge. But as many of us know from experience, holidays can turn into a time of stress and excess—too much food, too much shopping, too much to do, and too much waste. The US Environmental Protection Agency estimates that household trash increases 25 percent between Thanksgiving and Christmas in the United States. With decorations, gifts, parties, and extravagant feasts, it's easy to go overboard and overstuff your garbage bin. But with the right mind-set, and a little planning, we can simplify and get back to the good stuff. Here are a few simple ways to stay festive while keeping waste to a minimum.

**Decor.** Decorating without waste is easy, just look to nature for inspiration. In winter, deck your home with evergreen garlands and wreaths, strings of cranberries, dried orange slices, and popcorn. Add a homemade gingerbread house if you're feeling *extra*. For spring, think local flowers—daffodils, cherry blossom branches, and any other blooms you can forage. For summer holidays like Fourth of July, try edible decorations—load your table with watermelon slices, icy pitchers of lemonade, and strawberry shortcake topped with whipped cream. For fall holidays, use pumpkins and gourds that can be reused to make soups and treats. The best part about decorating with nature is, once you're done, everything can go in the compost—no more bulky plastic bins full of seasonal decor taking up valuable space in the garage.

**Candles.** Complement decor with a few unscented candles made from sustainably sourced beeswax or soy wax; same goes for lighting the menorah.

**Gifts.** An easy way to minimize holiday waste is by giving experience gifts, like tickets to a concert, sporting event, movie, museum, cooking class, yoga or meditation workshop, or spa treatment, or a digital gift certificate to a favorite restaurant. If you're looking for something tangible, give homemade brownies, cookies, jams, candied nuts, granola, bath salts, and candles in an upcycled jar or metal tin. If you're short on time or don't feel like crafting or baking, visit the bulk aisle and fill up a glass jar with bulk chocolates, candy, coffee beans, loose-leaf tea, toffee nuts, and honey, or visit your favorite local winery or brewery to fill up a reusable growler. You can also buy gifts secondhand or give reusable supplies to help nudge someone you love to ditch disposables (*hint, hint*).

If you anticipate receiving gifts, being proactive is key. Be open about your zero-waste lifestyle and offer concrete suggestions, like that refillable pen you've had your eye on.

**Gift wrap.** Always reuse what you have for wrapping gifts—paper bags, newspaper, an old map, or calendar all work well and look great. You could also use reusable cloth gift bags, or hide the surprise in a gift itself like a linen tea towel, tote bag, or scarf. A furoshiki cloth is a great way to deliver a bottle of wine and is a versatile kitchen tool—from a dish towel to an apron to a casserole carrier. Secure packages with reused ribbons or compostable kitchen twine. Avoid buying gift wrap with glitter, foil, velvet, and other synthetic embellishments because it can only be reused, not recycled.

**Knickknacks.** If the holidays aren't complete without a Santa figurine or dreidel, try buying them secondhand and favor sustainable materials such as wood, glass, metal, ceramic, and cotton.

**Twinkle lights.** Repair broken strands of twinkle lights or recycle them at Home Depot or Lowe's. If you're buying new lights, opt for LED or solar versions.

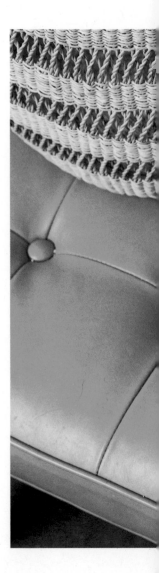

# THE HOLIDAYS: DOS AND DON'TS

✓ **Do** use nature as inspiration for decor—incorporate local foliage, evergreen garlands, and pumpkins.

✓ **Do** repurpose paper bags, newspaper, and calendars to wrap gifts.

✓ **Do** gift treats that are homemade or goodies purchased in bulk in a reusable jar.

✗ **Don't** be tempted by discount decor at big retail stores; make your own or buy it secondhand.

✗ **Don't** recycle gift wrap with glitter, foil, or embellishments—reuse it or throw it away.

✗ **Don't** expect friends and family to know what counts as a zero-waste gift—drop a hint, or two.

# Check Out My Zero-Waste Dinner Party

1.  **Think seasonal.** Build your meal around seasonal foods to keep flavors fresh and reduce waste.

2.  **Think reusable.** Real plates, cutlery, and cloth napkins add elegance to the table and help keep waste to a minimum.

3.  **Think bulk.** Appetizers such as olives, nuts, and dried fruit are bought in bulk in reusable glass jars and cloth bags.

4.  **Think one pot.** Cook and serve the meal in a cast-iron skillet or Dutch oven to simplify cooking and reduce the number of dishes washed.

5.  **Think local.** Beverages include local wine and filtered tap water with lemon slices served from a glass carafe.

# 5 Zero-Waste Tips for Entertaining

The best dinner parties revolve around good company and hearty meals (and wine, *lots* of wine). After a few disasters, I've learned to ditch fussy recipes in favor of simple crowd-pleasers I'd make on a typical weeknight. To save time and reduce dishwashing, aim for a one-pot meal or casserole that can be served straight onto plates. Better yet, make it a day ahead so flavors can build overnight and you can relax before guests arrive (or frantically clean, if you're like me).

1. **Tap will do.** Serve tap water from a glass bottle or carafe and add lemon, fruit, or cucumber slices if you want to get *schmancy*. You could also serve one or two bottles of sparkling water or make your own if you have a soda maker. Consider filling a reusable growler from your favorite local winery or craft brewery. For daytime parties, make a large pitcher of cold brew coffee with a reusable cloth filter the night before.

2. **Ditch disposables.** Nothing complements a beautiful home-cooked meal like ceramic plates, real flatware, and cloth napkins. Your table will look picture perfect with minimal effort. Plastic utensils and paper plates might seem more convenient, especially when hosting a large group, or maybe you don't have place settings for more than four people. Make it collaborative and have guests bring extra plates, cutlery, and napkins, or borrow from a neighbor or friend. If you want to use single-use plates, opt for compostable paper or bamboo over plastic.

3. **Get your compost ready.** It's always nice (and polite) when guests offer to help with cleanup after a decadent meal. Be sure to have your compost bin out and clearly labeled so guests know where to put their scraps. Make an announcement as dinner winds down: "The compost bin is in the kitchen. Please clear your plate so we can get ready for dessert."

4. **Avoid gimmicks.** While Peeps bunnies and Valentine's Day heart candy can be festive and cute, try to avoid the plastic-packaged "extras" sold during the holidays. Instead, incorporate seasonal ingredients into meals, or if you want to get kitschy, pick up a Yule log cake or Star of David cookies from your local bakery in your own container.

5. **BYO container.** One of the best parts of a big meal is leftovers. You probably cooked more than you need and don't want it to go to waste. Instead of sending guests home with plastic baggies, ask them to bring storage containers from home or repurpose containers from your recycling bin. Freeze some leftovers right away, so you don't get sick of eating the same thing too many days in a row.

**HOSTESS GIFTS**

Heading to a party and don't want to come empty-handed? My favorite hostess gifts are local flowers wrapped in paper, small houseplants propagated from clippings, wood cooking spoons, and linen dish towels.

## You Can Compost That

- Christmas tree

- Crepe paper streamers

- Evergreen garlands (wires removed)

- Envelopes

- Greeting cards (without photos, glitter, or embellishment)

- Halloween pumpkins

- Holiday wreaths (wires removed)

- Kitchen twine

- Latex balloons

- Masking tape

- Paper gift wrap (without glitter, velvet, or embellishments)

- Tissue paper

# Plastic-Free(ish) Action Plan

| SMALL WINS | BIG WINS |
|---|---|
| • Buy clothes made from natural or recycled fabrics from ethical businesses.<br><br>• Donate clothing and shoes that are in good condition.<br><br>• Bring a reusable water bottle when traveling.<br><br>• Download your boarding pass onto your phone to skip the paper ticket.<br><br>• Switch to compostable plates and cutlery for large holiday gatherings and parties. | • Buy clothes, shoes, and accessories secondhand from thrift stores or online.<br><br>• Recycle damaged textiles and shoes and sell valuable pieces.<br><br>• Pack your own meal, cutlery, and napkin for waste-free travel.<br><br>• Limit yourself to one carry-on to reduce carbon emissions, and skip plastic luggage tags.<br><br>• Use real plates, cutlery, and napkins for low-waste entertaining. |

# Final Thoughts

I'm so grateful to write about a topic that brings me joy and to share the tips and practices that have helped our family curb plastic waste. And yet, to be fully transparent, I've struggled with my inner critic throughout this writing process; it reminds me that I am neither an expert on zero-waste nor plastic-free lifestyles. There are already dozens of resources that detail how to live with zero waste, primarily by women who claim to fit all their yearly trash into a single Mason jar. Although I now produce minimal waste compared to what I used to, I'm still learning to balance this lifestyle and grow a business with my husband, care for a toddler, *and* carve out "me" time. For the most part, I've found that adopting zero-waste principles has made my life simpler and less chaotic, but some days are more wasteful than others and there are times when I prioritize self-care over an empty trash bin.

What's kept me motivated to share my story is the encouragement from friends, family, my publishing team, and readers of the *Wild Minimalist* blog. I've been reminded that people appreciate hearing from someone who is doing their best to live more sustainably, but doesn't *quite* have it all figured out. The truth is, I think most people (especially women) already have too much pressure to be perfect—to have a thriving career, keep a spotless home, and be a super parent, with a perfect body and ageless skin . . . and let's just add making all your own food, beauty, and cleaning supplies from scratch, and producing zero-plastic waste in the process. *That* is unsustainable. I hope to make zero-waste lifestyles more accessible and less scary to someone just starting out, and lessen this pressure to do it all perfectly.

I've also heard the zero-waste movement can be elitist and expensive—who's going to spend $20 on reusable beeswax cloths when a roll of plastic cling wrap costs just under $2.50? Although I could argue that the up front cost of reusable products will pay for itself over time, while protecting the environment, I understand and acknowledge this is a privileged view. We all have varying levels of resources available that affect a zero-waste lifestyle, be it money, time, community support, reusable supplies, or access to bulk stores. My recommendation is to do the best you can with what's available without driving yourself crazy in the process. It's important to note that many people and cultures around the world already practice being resourceful and minimizing waste without identifying their lifestyle as "zero waste." Really, Western society is playing catch-up and leveraging the practices used by older generations and Indigenous cultures worldwide.

My goal with this book is to help motivate more people to adopt a *mostly* plastic-free lifestyle and to do it in a way that's manageable and fun. Trash jars have been a powerful symbol for the zero-waste movement (they certainly shocked and inspired me many years ago), but they can also be limiting and exclusionary. I want readers to feel encouraged by their progress, to celebrate the wins, and not to feel discouraged or ashamed if they can't fit their yearly waste into a Mason jar. For our family, going plastic free has been a gradual process of replacing disposable products with something sustainable, or finding a way to do without. And through that process, we have become more mindful and resourceful, while discovering unexpected joy in minimalism and simplicity.

We can all be better at reducing plastic waste and protecting the environment. I believe every person can play an important role in the zero-waste movement and that each small action will help shift society in a positive direction. The more we come together and encourage one another to refuse disposable products, the more our business leaders, politicians, and peers will listen. Thank you for letting me be part of your journey toward a low-waste lifestyle and please remember to celebrate every small step along the way. You're doing great.

# Plastic-Free(ish) Resources

## RECYCLING RESOURCES

Part of reducing waste is finding a way to divert items you'd normally throw away. First, check with your local waste department to see what materials they accept in your curbside recycling and compost bins. Then, check to see whether they offer a drop-off for hard-to-recycle items like cooking oil, hazardous waste, prescription medicine, etc. Here are a few additional locations that accept donations, drop-offs, or postal delivery of hard-to-recycle items.

**#5 plastic.** Whole Foods Market (check with your local store)

**Arts and crafts supplies.** Donate to a local preschool or elementary school.

**Batteries (rechargeable).** Ace Hardware, Home Depot, Lowe's, Staples, Walgreens

**Batteries (single use).** Ace Hardware, IKEA, Lowe's, Target, Walgreens

**Bras.** Free the Girls, Donate Your Bra, I Support the Girls, The Bra Recyclers

**Christmas lights.** Ace Hardware, Goodwill, Home Depot, Lowe's, Salvation Army, Walmart

**Clothing.** Eileen Fisher (its brand only), Goodwill, H&M, Levi's (any brand of jeans), Madewell (any brand of jeans), Patagonia (its brand only), Salvation Army, North Face, Uniqlo

**Compact fluorescent lightbulbs.** Ace Hardware, Home Depot, IKEA, Lowe's

**Contact lenses and blister packs.** Mail to TerraCycle.

**Cooking oil.** Contact your local waste department to find a drop-off.

**Corks.** BevMo!

**Electronic waste.** Best Buy, Goodwill, Staples, Target

**Expired car seats.** Target (check with your local store)

**Eyeglasses.** Goodwill, LensCrafters, Lions Club, New Eyes for the Needy, OneSight, Salvation Army

**Gift cards.** Mail to TerraCycle.

**Ink cartridges.** Best Buy, Office Depot, Office Max, Staples

**Makeup.** M•A•C Cosmetics (its brand only), Origins (any brand)

**Medicine.** CVS Pharmacy, Walgreens

**Packing peanuts and bubble wrap.** UPS (some stores)

**Paint.** Ace Hardware, Kelly-Moore, Sherwin-Williams

**Pens.** Mail to TerraCycle.

**Pet items.** Contact your local animal shelter or rescue.

**Plastic bags and film (aka soft plastics).** Enter your zip code at PlasticFilmRecycling.com to find drop-off locations near you.

**Plastic plant pots.** Home Depot, Lowe's

**Razors, blades, and packaging.** Mail to TerraCycle.

**Scrap metal.** Find a scrap metal yard.

**Shoes.** Converse (any brand of athletic shoes in any condition), Goodwill (any type of shoe in any condition), Nike (any brand of athletic shoes in any condition), Salvation Army, Vans (its brand only)

**Textiles (any condition).** Goodwill, H&M, Salvation Army

**Toothbrushes, toothpaste tubes, floss containers (plastic).** Mail to TerraCycle.

**Tyvek envelopes.** Mail to DuPont.

---

## COMPOST RESOURCES

Whether you have outdoor space or live in a tiny apartment, whether you want to be super hands on or hands off, there are many ways to compost organic materials and reduce household waste. Here are a few different compost methods to help you decide which option is right for you.

### Community Composting Methods

**Curbside.** If you're not interested in managing a home compost system, ask whether your local waste department accepts food scraps and other organic materials. Be sure to note which items they accept, as guidelines will vary.

**Drop-off.** If your city doesn't provide a compost service, look for a local drop-off. Many farmers' markets offer one, but you can also look for a community garden, local farm, or neighbor with chickens. You can also type your location into ShareWaste.com to find a nearby drop-off.

# Home Composting Methods

| Method | Description | Cost | |
|--------|-------------|------|---|
| **INDOOR** | | | |
| **Bokashi** | Developed in Japan, the Bokashi method ferments food scraps and other organic materials. You simply layer food scraps with a special bran material in a Bokashi bucket. The bucket has an airtight lid and a tap at the bottom to drain off "Bokashi tea," a liquid that can be used to fertilize plants. | You can make your own bucket or buy one from between $60 and $150. You also have to buy or make the Bokashi bran on an ongoing basis. | |
| **Electric composter** | An electric composter is a sleek enclosed bin that turns food scraps into compost in as little as three hours. The system uses agitators and heat to break down and dehydrate organic matter to produce a material that can be added directly to your garden. | $350 (for the FoodCycler) | |
| **Worm farm** | To create a worm farm, also known as vermi-composting, you layer food scraps and brown materials like newspaper and cardboard in a bin and just add worms (red wigglers, to be exact!). Worms can eat half their weight in food every day and produce beneficial castings (aka worm manure) that add rich nutrients to soil and plants. | You can make your own bin or buy one from between $20 and $180. You also have to factor in the cost of worms. | |
| **OUTDOOR** | | | |
| **Closed bin** | A closed bin is typically a square or cylindrical bin with a lid and no bottom, often made from recycled plastic. You add food scraps and other organics to the pile at the top and either turn the contents manually with a shovel from the top or move the entire bin to a new location to harvest the compost material inside. | You can make your own or buy one for between $80 and $200. | |
| **Open bin** | An open compost bin is a structured area, generally made from wire or wood fencing, where you place food scraps and other organic materials. Unlike a closed bin, the open bin has no lid so the composting material can be turned easily by shovel to speed decomposition. | Cost of materials, or buy premade for between $50 and $150. | |
| **Trench** | When trench, or pit, composting, you fill a hole with organic waste and bury it with soil. That's it—naturally occurring worms and bacteria break down the waste and add nutrients to the soil. | Get a shovel and dig—no extra cost. | |
| **Tumbler** | A tumbler composter is a raised drum to which you add food and other organic material and turn by handle or hand. Turning the contents of your tumbler introduces oxygen to help speed up the decomposition process. | Make your own or buy one for between $100 and $300. | |

| Time | Pros | Cons |
|------|------|------|
| Two weeks until compost is fermented, then it has to be added to conventional compost to decompose further. | It's odorless and compact, and you can compost dairy, meat, and other scraps that can't be added to most other compost methods. | Produces a fermented byproduct, not compost material, that has to be buried in a trench or added to a conventional compost before it's ready to be added to plants. |
| About three hours | It's odorless, compact, and requires very little effort. It's also fast and can be used for dairy, meat, and greasy foods. | One of the most expensive methods available and, like all tech gadgets, there's always the possibility that it will break. |
| Three to six months until you're able to harvest. | Doesn't take up much space and, if you do it right, it's odorless. Produces a nutrient-rich fertilizer that can be added directly to plants. | Worms are like pets and need the right conditions (temperature, moisture, oxygen) and the proper type and quantity of foods to stay healthy. You can't feed them citrus, meat, dairy, garlic, onion, or spicy or greasy foods. |
| Six months to one year | Keeps the compost pile contained and helps prevent pests. | Can be difficult to access the compost and might take a long time until harvest. Can't add meat, dairy, or greasy foods. |
| If you turn your pile often, it can take as little as three weeks. | Bins are inexpensive to build and can accommodate large volumes. They can also be turned more easily than a closed bin to speed harvest time. | Can take up a lot of space and attract pests. Can't add meat, dairy, or greasy foods. |
| Six months to one year | Easy, cheap, and pest resistant. Works with meat and dairy. | You have to dig a pretty deep hole and you can't easily transport the compost material. It's best to dig the trench right where you plan to grow. |
| Three to six weeks | Because the compost is contained, it's fairly tidy and compact and helps keep out pests. | Can be expensive and the volume is limited. You should not add dairy, meat, or greasy foods. |

## You Can Compost That

People often associate composting with food scraps, aka "greens." But did you know that balancing your greens with "browns," like newspaper and dead leaves, is essential for decomposition? Greens are nitrogen-rich materials that attract microorganisms to heat up the pile, whereas browns are carbon-rich materials that feed the microorganisms and add bulk to the pile to promote airflow. Aim for a ratio of three to four parts browns to one part greens, but it doesn't have to be exact and can be adjusted as needed. Luckily, our homes produce an abundance of greens and browns daily that will convert your compost pile into black gold for the garden.

### GREENS

- Coffee grounds
- Eggshells
- Flowers
- Fruit and vegetable scraps
- Grass clippings
- Hair, fur, feathers
- Herbivore pet dropping (chickens, hamsters, rabbits)
- Houseplant clippings
- Loose-leaf tea
- Nail clippings (human and pet)
- Nutshells
- Seaweed and algae

### BROWNS

- Cardboard (cereal boxes, donut boxes, egg cartons, pizza boxes)
- Coffee filters
- Cork
- Cotton products (balls, facial rounds, swabs)
- Dead tree leaves, branches, pinecones, pine needles
- Dryer lint
- Latex (balloons and gloves)
- Mail (catalogs, envelopes)
- Newspaper
- Natural loofah and sea sponges
- Natural rope and twine
- Natural fabric (bamboo, cotton, hemp, linen, silk, wool cut into small pieces)
- Paper products (cupcake wrappers, bags, napkins, plates, towels)
- Paper tea bags (with staple removed)
- Silk dental floss
- Straw and hay
- Tissue paper
- Toilet paper and cardboard tubes
- Untreated wood (dish brush, sawdust, skewers, toothbrush handle, toothpicks)
- Vacuum contents and broom sweepings
- Wood ashes

## You Can't Compost That

- Charcoal ashes (from chemically treated briquettes; wood charcoal is fine)
- Compostable diapers +
- Compostable plastics +
- Dairy products*
- Dog and cat poo (try a worm farm)
- Fats and cooking oils*
- Meat, fish, and bones*
- Plants sprayed with pesticides/herbicides
- Treated wood
- Weeds*

\* okay in Bokashi, electric composter, and some curbside green bins

\+ only through an industrial composting facility; check curbside program or find a designated service

## BUYING RESOURCES

From clothing to furniture to electronics, there are many opportunities to shop more sustainably. In this buying resources guide, I've included the best websites for scoring consignment and vintage items, as well as my favorite plastic-free brands for the kitchen, bath, cleaning, and more. Although the best way to reduce waste is to limit shopping, my hope is that this guide will help you feel better about your purchases when you do need essentials (or a little something extra).

## Online Resources to Buy-Sell-Trade Secondhand Items

**Craigslist.** Find secondhand furniture, electronics, sports equipment, and more, sold locally.

**eBay.** Search for used clothing, shoes, and household items.

**Etsy.** Find a variety of housewares, toys, clothing, and other vintage items.

**Facebook.** Check out the marketplace and buy-sell-trade groups.

**Nextdoor.** Find furniture, garden supplies, and household items sold (or sometimes offered for free) by neighbors.

**OfferUp:** Another option for buying and selling secondhand items locally.

**Poshmark.** Find used clothing, shoes, and accessories for the whole family.

**The RealReal.** Find luxury consignment clothing, shoes, and accessories.

**thredUP.** Find used clothes, shoes, handbags, and more.

**Tradesy.** For luxury consignment clothes, shoes, accessories, and even wedding dresses.

# Before you buy something new, ask yourself . . .

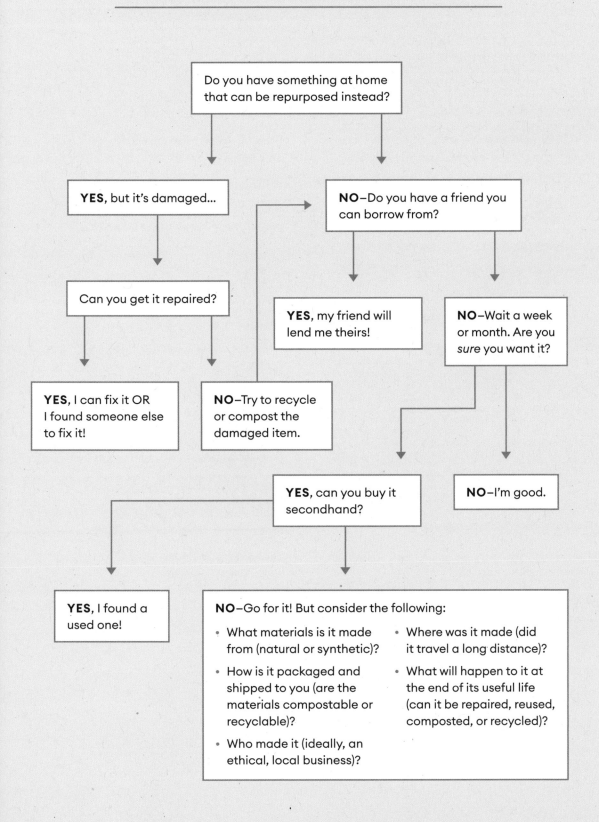

# Brands I Love

## CLEANING

**Dropps.** Laundry and dishwasher detergent pods mailed in a recyclable cardboard box

**Fillaree.** Dish and hand soap sold in glass bottles with refill options

**Marley's Monsters.** Reusable cloth baby wipes, facial rounds, unpaper towels, and more

**Meliora.** Powdered laundry detergent in refillable metal containers

**Redecker.** Cleaning brushes, brooms, copper scrubbers, and other household items

**Woolzies.** Wool dryer balls

## KITCHEN AND DINING

**Ambatalia.** Linen utensil wraps, bowl covers, bento bags, furoshiki cloths

**Bee's Wrap.** Compostable wraps for saving food and covering bowls

**Bormioli Rocco.** Airtight latch-top jars for storing food

**CoffeeSock.** Reusable cloth filters for brewing coffee, tea, and nut milk

**Dans le Sac.** Reusable cotton bread bags

**Eco-Bags.** Mesh and muslin produce bags

**KeepCup.** Glass to-go coffee cups

**Klean Kanteen.** Stainless-steel water bottles

**Le Parfait.** Airtight latch-top jars for storing food

**Meema.** Upcycled cotton dish towels, napkins, and aprons

**Onyx Containers.** Stainless-steel containers, ice packs, and ice cube trays

**Stasher.** Reusable silicone bags

**The Swag.** Cotton storage bags that help produce last longer

**To-Go Ware.** Stainless-steel tiffins, bamboo to-go utensils

You can find many of these low-waste essentials at **Wild Minimalist,** our online and retail store.

## BATH AND BEAUTY

**Blade + Bloom.** Natural, plant-based skincare sold in recyclable or reusable containers

**Brush Naked.** Compostable bamboo toothbrushes

**Chagrin Valley Soap & Salve.** Bar soaps, shampoo bars, bug repellent sticks, and more, sold in cardboard boxes and tubes

**Dot Cup.** Reusable menstrual cup

**Elate Cosmetics.** Natural makeup in sustainable packaging

**Fat and the Moon.** Makeup, lotion, balms, and serums, sold in recyclable packaging

**Georganics.** Silk dental floss, toothpaste, and mouthwash tablets, sold in glass jars

**jELN.** Plant-based self care essentials sold in recyclable glass containers

**KOOSHOO.** Compostable hair ties and scrunchies

**Meow Meow Tweet.** Vegan soaps, shampoo bars, deodorant, and more, sold in compostable and recyclable packaging

**PATCH.** Compostable bamboo bandages

**Raw Elements.** Sunscreen sold in metal tins

**Rockwell Razors.** Classic safety razors

**Smartliners.** Reusable cotton underwear liners and period pads

## CLOTHING

**Christy Dawn.** Dresses made from recycled textiles

**Girlfriend Collective.** Athletic apparel made from recycled water bottles

**Patagonia.** Outdoor apparel made from recycled gear

**Proclaim.** Bras and undies made from Tencel and recycled water bottles

## Reading I Recommend

**Bea Johnson.** *Zero Waste Home* (Scribner, 2013)

**Carolyn Finney.** *Black Faces, White Spaces* (UNC Press, 2014)

**Julia Watkins.** *Simply Living Well* (Houghton Mifflin Harcourt, 2020)

**Leah Thomas et al.** The Intersectional Environmentalist (https://www. intersectionalenvironmentalist.com)

**Marie Kondo.** *The Life-Changing Magic of Tidying Up* (Ten Speed Press, 2014)

**Rachel Carson.** *Silent Spring* (Houghton Mifflin Harcourt, 2002)

# References and Further Reading

Borunda, Alejandra, in partnership with the National Geographic Society. "How Tampons and Pads Became So Unsustainable." *National Geographic* (September 6, 2019). NationalGeographic.com /environment/2019/09/how-tampons-pads-became-unsustainable-story-of-plastic/.

Breastcancer.org. "Exposure to Chemicals in Plastic." Breastcancer.org /risk/factors/plastic.

Center for Urban Education and Sustainable Agriculture (CUESA). "How Far Does Your Food Travel to Get to Your Plate?" CUESA.org/learn/how-far-does-your-food-travel-get-your-plate.

Cox, Kieran D., Garth Covernton, Hailey Davies, John Dower, Francis Juanes, and Sarah Dudas. "Human Consumption of Microplastics." *Environmental Science & Technology* 53, no. 12 (June 5, 2019): 7068–7074. https://doi.org/10.1021/acs.est.9b01517.

Deprez, Esmé. "It's Tough Being the First Birth Control App," Bloomberg *BusinessWeek* (April 1, 2019). Bloomberg.com/news/features/2019-04-01 /birth-control-app-natural-cycles-is-more-effective-than-the-pill.

Doran, Grace, and Jessica Kidwell. "Creative Ways to Cut Your Holiday Waste." United States Environmental Protection Agency. *The EPA Blog*. blog.EPA.gov/2016/12/21/creative-ways-to-cut-your-holiday-waste.

Ellen MacArthur Foundation. "The New Plastics Economy–Rethinking the Future of Plastics." World Economic Forum (January 19, 2016): 7. EllenMacarthurFoundation.org/publications.

Geyer, Roland, Jenna Jameck, and Kara Lavender Law. "Production, Use, and Fate of All Plastics Ever Made." *Science Advances* 3, no. 7 (July 2017): e1700782. doi.org/10.1126/sciadv.1700782.

Gunders, Dana. "Wasted: How America Is Losing Up to 40 Percent of Its Food from Farm to Fork to Landfill." National Resources Defense Council (August 16, 2017). NRDC.org/resources/wasted-how-america-losing-40-percent-its-food-farm-fork-landfill.

Lebreton, L., B. Slat, F. Ferrari, et al. "Evidence that the Great Pacific Garbage Patch Is Rapidly Accumulating Plastic." *Scientific Reports* 8, no. 4666 (March 22, 2018). https://doi.org/10.1038/s41598-018-22939-w.

Moore, Charles. Algalita Marine Research Foundation, presentation at California District Attorney's Association (September 2006).

Morris, William. *Hopes and fears for art*. Longmans, Green, and Co, 1901. https://library.si.edu/digital-library/book/hopesfearsforar00morr.

Plumer, Brad. "Plastic Bags, or Paper? Here's What to Consider When You Hit the Grocery Store." *New York Times* (March 29, 2019). NYTimes.com/2019/03/29/climate/plastic-paper-shopping-bags.html.

Siegle, Lucy. "The Eco Guide to Sanitary Products." *The Guardian* (October 2017). TheGuardian.com/environment/2017/oct/29/the-eco-guide-to-period-dramas.

United States Environmental Protection Agency. "Composting at Home." EPA.gov/recycle/composting-home.

United States Environmental Protection Agency. "Greenhouse Gas Emissions." EPA.gov/ghgemissions/overview-greenhouse-gases#CH4-reference.

United States Environmental Protection Agency. "Municipal Solid Waste." Archive.EPA.gov/epawaste/nonhaz/municipal/web/html.

United States Environmental Protection Agency. "National Overview: Facts and Figures on Materials, Wastes and Recycling." EPA.gov/facts-and-figures-about-materials-waste-and-recycling/national-overview-facts-and-figures-materials.

United States Environmental Protection Agency. "Sustainable Management of Food Basics. EPA.gov/sustainable-management-food/sustainable-management-food-basics.

Weiss, Kenneth. "Altered Oceans: Part Four: Plague of Plastic Chokes the Seas." *Los Angeles Times* (August 2, 2006). LATimes.com/world/la-me-ocean2aug02-story.html.

Wicker, Alden. "Fast Fashion Is Creating an Environmental Crisis." *Newsweek* (September 1, 2016). Newsweek.com/2016/09/09/old-clothes-fashion-waste-crisis-494824.html.

# Acknowledgments

Thank you to the entire Ten Speed Press team for bringing this book to life. To Hannah Rahill for sparking the idea and guiding me through the proposal. To my editor, Shaida Boroumand, for your wisdom and reassurance at every step in this process. To Kelly Booth, for braving a pandemic to manage a wildly ambitious photoshoot. And to Lisa Bieser, for your patience and care in crafting these beautiful pages.

To Aubrie Pick, for elevating my words through your stunning photography, and Suzie Holmstrom for prop styling and attention to detail. To Sarah Bonar and her family for graciously opening their beautiful home for the photoshoot.

To my husband/business partner/co-parenter, Max, thank you for taking our son on countless adventures so I could finish writing, for picking up the slack at home and work so I could focus, and being my all around support system whenever I feel overwhelmed or anxious. Our relationship mantra, "headfirst swan dive," has led to more beauty and fulfillment than I could ever imagine. And to my son, for your patience and love while mama wrote.

To my father, Mickey, thank you for igniting my love and appreciation of nature at an early age—from hikes in a baby backpack, to rollerblading trips along the California coast, and foregoing traditional Thanksgiving plans for adventures in Yosemite and Sequoia. You've always led by example and demonstrated how to be resourceful and mindful—inspiring me to better care for my health, surroundings, and loved ones.

To my ride or die friends, I am beyond blessed to have you in my life. Your unconditional love and support mean the world to me. And finally, a huge thanks to the readers and supporters of Wild Minimalist and the zero waste community. You are a continual source of inspiration and encouragement, and I truly believe we are on the path to a better future.

# Index

Library of Congress Cataloging-in-Publication Data
Names: Cameron, Lily, 1986– author.
Title: Simply sustainable : moving toward plastic-free, low-waste living /
    Lily Cameron.
Description: First edition. | Emeryville : Ten Speed Press, [2020] |
    Includes bibliographical references.
Identifiers: LCCN 2020026853 (print) | LCCN 2020026854 (ebook) |
    ISBN 9781984859136 (trade paperback) | ISBN 9781984859143 (ebook)
Subjects: LCSH: Sustainable living. | Plastics–Environmental aspects. |
    Waste minimization.
Classification: LCC GE196 .C34 2020 (print) | LCC GE196 (ebook) |
    DDC 640.28/6–dc23
LC record available at https://lccn.loc.gov/2020026853
LC ebook record available at https://lccn.loc.gov/2020026854

Hardcover ISBN: 978-1-9848-5913-6
eBook ISBN: 978-1-9848-5914-3

Printed in Italy

Acquiring editor: Hannah Rahill
Project editor: Shaida Boroumand
Designer: Lisa Schneller Bieser
Art director: Kelly Booth
Production designers: Mari Gill
    and Mara Gendell
Production manager: Dan Myers
Prepress color manager: Jane Chinn

Photo assistant: Patrick Aguilar
Food & prop stylist: Suzie Holmstrom
Prop assistant: Erin Bronowich
Copyeditor: Mary Cassells
Proofreader: Linda Bouchard
Indexer: Ken DellaPenta
Publicist: Jana Branson
Marketer: Monica Stanton

10 9 8 7 6 5 4 3 2 1

First Edition